OPTIONS TRADING

The Beginners Guide to Invest and Make a Passive Income & The Best Strategies to Maximize The Profit

Anthony Price

Table of Contents:

Introduction

If you are reading this book now, it means you have taken an interesting ride through the world of options trading. We know you are wondering why you didn't know such attractive investment opportunity till now. Or maybe you've heard about it, but it seemed all complicated then. And now, all you want to do is dive headlong into the sea of options. Hey, relax. There are other lessons you need to know. We don't want you losing money.

There are guides you need to follow to ensure you are trading right. Options are easy and flexible, yet a little misstep can cost you a lot. So here are some tips to guide you:

—In trading options, you are making predictions. It is like forecasting theweather: the forecaster observes the elements and tells whether it will rain or snow. But on some days these forecasts may be wrong. So, there is always room for uncertainty. Your predictions aren't foolproof. Always know thatthe market can swing against your prediction. Don't trust your expectationsso much that you place a huge bet on the trade. It is true that investments come with risks, but the goal is to avoid or minimize losses.

—Always remember that the value of options is tied to the underlying asset. And the stock market is a very volatile one. The value of the underlying asset is governed by demand and supply; it is never constant. Therefore, it is important you study the trends (historical volatility) before purchasing an option. Also learn to anticipate the news. There is a mantra for this: "Buy the rumor, sell the news." Investopedia stated an interesting fact: "Wall Street traders don't try to follow the news. They try to anticipate it." The reason for this is simple: news can increase or decrease the demand foran asset, thus making the value of the asset skyrocket or plummet.

News can either be bad or good. If it is bad the stock price falls. An example of bad news includes a bad earnings report. Good news such as a merger/acquisition, new product release or good earnings report, increases the value of stock. So good traders don't wait for the news, they source for it before it is announced. They stay informed. For instance, an investor may have a hint that Microsoft will make a new acquisition, so he decides to purchase a call option because he knows that when the news drops, demand increases and then he makes profit. But if the same investor gets the rumor that there is a huge drop in the revenue of Facebook, he may decide to purchase a put option in order to profit from the price drop when the earnings report is published.

Furthermore, be conversant with global socioeconomic climate. Be aware of new or modified policies and how they affect a company. Do not take option positions without knowing everything going on around the stock. Stay informed always. This leads to the next point.

—Belong to a community. Do not trade alone. The financial world is a huge community often made up of smaller communities. In these communities, there are CEOS, investors, venture capitalists, entrepreneurs, and so on. All these people are interested in how stocks perform. Information circulate within these communities, and if you are a lone trader you would definitely miss out. You can only buy the rumor when you hear about it. And you can't hear a rumor when you are not within a community. Also, being part of a community gives you further insights concerning trading options. You get new ideas and perspectives that you may not have seen before.

Social media has made being part of a trading community easy. There are open and closed Facebook, WhatsApp, and Telegram groups were trading information and the performance of the market are shared. You can also follow trading or investment bigwigs on their social media platforms. These individuals usually share what they think about the market or a stock. In fact, rumors spring from them.

—The stock market or options market is not like a shopping mall. In a shopping mall, no one loses. The buyer pays for the products they need. The seller accepts money they also need. It is a win-win for both parties. But inthe stock market or options market, a trader's loss is another's gain. This is a fundamental principle you need bear in mind as you trade. An option that is profitable to you is unprofitable to another trader. When you purchase a call option expecting the value of the stock to increase, the call writer is expectingthe value to decrease. It is a game. A clash of expectations. And you must endeavor not to be on the losing side. Be smart with your investment. Trade intelligently.

Chapter 1: What is Options Contract?

An options contract sounds fancy, but it's a pretty simple concept.

It's a contract. That means it's a legal agreement between a buyer and   a seller.

It gives the purchaser of the contract the opportunity to purchase ordispose of an asset with a fixed amount.

The purchase is optional – so the buyer of the contract does not have to buy or sell the asset.

The contract has an expiration date, so the purchaser – if they choose to exercise their right – must make the trade on or before the expiration date.

The purchaser of the contract pays a non-refundable fee for the contract.

While the focus of this book is on options contracts related to the stock market, there are options contracts that take place in all aspects of daily life, including real estate and speculation. A simple example illustrates the concept of an options contract.

Suppose you are itching to buy a BMW, and you've decided the model you want must be silver. You drop by a local dealer, and it turns out they don't have a silver model in stock. The dealer claims he can get you one by the end of the month. You say you'll take the car if the dealer can get it bythe last day of the month, and he'll sell it to you for $67,500. He agrees and requires you to put a $3,000 deposit on the car.

If the last day of the month arrives and the dealer hasn't produced the car, then you're freed from the contract and get your money back. In the event he does produce the car at any date before the end of the month, you have the option to buy it or not. If you really wanted the car you can buy it, but of course, you can't be forced to buy the car, and maybe you've changed your mind in the interim.

The right is there but not the obligation to purchase, in short, no pressure if you decided not to push through with the purchase of the car. If you decide to let the opportunity pass, however, since the dealer met his end of the bargain and produced the car, you lose the $3,000 deposit.

In this case, the dealer, who plays the role of the writer of the contract, has the obligation to follow through with the sale based upon the agreed-uponprice.

Suppose that when the car arrives at the dealership, BMW announces it will no longer make silver cars. As a result, prices of new silver BMWs that was the last ones to roll off the assembly line skyrocket. Other dealers are selling their silver BMWs for $100,000. However, since this dealer entered into an options contract with you, then he must sell the car to you for the pre- agreed price of $67,500. You decide to get the car and drive away, smiling, knowing that you saved $32,500 and that you could sell it at a profit if you wanted to.

The situation here is capturing the essence of options contracts, even if you've never thought of haggling with a car dealer in those terms.

An option is, in a sense, a kind of bet. In the example of the car, the bet is that the dealer can produce the exact car you want within the specified time period and at the agreed-upon price. The dealer is betting too. His bet is that the pre-agreed to price is a good one for him. Of course, if BMW stops making silver cars, then he's made the wrong bet.

It can work the other way too. Let's say that instead of BMW deciding not to make silver cars anymore when your car is being driven onto the lot, another car crashes into it. Now your silver BMW has a small dent on the rear bumper with some scratches. As a result, the car has immediately declined in value. But if you want the car, since you've agreed to the options contract, you must pay $67,500, even though with the dent, it's only really worth $55,000. You can walk away and lose your $3,000 or pay what is nowa premium price on a damaged car.

Another example that is commonly used to explain options contracts isthe purchase of a home to be built by a developer under the agreement that certain conditions are met. The buyer will be required to put a non-refundable down payment or deposit on the home. Let's say that the developer agrees to build them the home for $300,000, provided that a new school is built within 5 miles of the development within one year. So, the contract expires within a year. At any time during the year, the buyer has the option to go forward with the construction of the home for $300,000 if the school is built. The developer has agreed to the price no matter what. So if the housing market in general and the construction of the school, in particular, drive up demand for housing in the area, and the developer is selling new homes that are now priced at $500,000, he has to sell this home for $300,000 because that was theprice agreed to when the contract was signed.

The home buyer got what they wanted, being within 5 miles of the new school, with the home price fixed at $300,000. The developer was assured of the sale but missed out on the unknown, which was the skyrocketing price that occurred as a result of increased demand. On the other hand, if the schoolisn't built and the buyers don't exercise their option to buy the house before the contract expires at one year, the developer can pocket the $20,000 cash.

What is an options contract on the stock market?

The same thing happens in the stock market. Of course in the case of the car, the buyer is simply hoping to get the car they want at what they perceive to be a bargain price, although if BMW really stopped making silver cars, they might sell it to a third party and then get a white one from the dealer. However, in most cases, the buyer wants the car. That isn't the case when it comes to options with stocks.

On the stock market, we are betting on the future price itself, and the shares of stock will be bought or sold at a profit if things work out. The key point is the buyer of the options contract is not hoping to acquire the shares and hold them for a long time period like a traditional investor.

Instead, you're hoping to make a bet on the price of the stock, secure that price, and then be able to trade the shares on that price no matter what happens on the actual markets. We will illustrate this with an example.

CALL Options

A call is a type of options contract that provides the option to purchase an asset at the agreed-upon amount at the designated time or deadline. The reason you would do this is if you felt that the price of a given stock would increase in price over the specified time period. Let's illustrate with anexample.

Suppose that Acme Communications makes cutting edge smartphones. The rumors are that they will announce a new smartphone in the next three weeks that is going to take the market by storm, with customers lined out the door to make preorders.

The current price that Acme Communications is trading at is $44.25 a share. The current pricing of an asset is termed as the spot price. Put another way; the spot price is the actual amount that you would be paying for the shares as you would buy it from the stock market right now.

Nobody really knows if the stock price will go up when the announcement is made, or if the announcement will even be made. But you've done your research and are reasonably confident these events will take place. You also have to estimate how much the shares will go up, and based on your research, you think it's going to shoot up to $65 a share by the end of the month.

You enter into an options contract for 100 shares at $1 per share. You pay this fee to the brokerage that is writing the options contract. In total, for 100 shares, you pay $100.

The price that is paid for an options contract is $100. This price is called the premium.

You don't get the premium back. It's a fee that you pay no matter what. If you make a profit, then it's all good. But if your bet is wrong, then you'll losethe premium. For the buyer of an options contract, the premium is their risk.

You'll want to set a price that you think is going to be lower than thelevel to which the price per share will rise. The price that you agree to is called the strike price. For this contract, you set your strike price at $50.

Remember, exercising your right to buy the shares is optional. You'll only buy the shares if the price goes high enough that you'll make a profit on the trade.

If the shares never go above $50, say they reach $48, you are not obligated to buy them. And why would you? As part of the contract deal, you'd be required to buy them at $50.

We'll say that the contract is entered on the 1st of August, and thedeadline is the third Friday in August. If the price goes higher than yourstrike price during that time, you can exercise your option.

Let's say that as the deadline approaches, things go basically as you planned.   Acme   Communications announces its new phone, and the stock starts climbing. The stock price on the actual market (the spot price) goes up to $60.

Now the seller is required to sell you the shares at $50 a share. You buy the shares, and then you can immediately dispose of these at a quality or optimal amount, or $60 a share. You make a profit of $10 a share, not taking into account any commissions or fees.

Chapter 2: Stock Options vs Index Options

Differences between index options and stock options

There are a couple of significant differences between stock options and index options. Let us take a closer look at some of these differences below.

• Stock options are traded and listed on the CBOE while index options are normally listed on the American Stock exchange, also known as Amex.

• Stock options are based on one company's stock and shares while index options are based on the shares of an entire spectrum of companies. The spectrum can be broad or narrow. Narrow indices are based on an individual sector such as semiconductors while broad based indices feature a whole variety of industries.

Stock options differ from index options due to the difference in the settlement methods. Index options are settled completely in monetary terms while stock options are settled using the underlying shares. Should you exercise an index option, you will be paid in cash.

• Stock options and index options differ in style. For instance, stock options feature American-style which means you are able to exercise them at any time before they expire. This is contrary to the index options which are European-style in nature. They can only be exercised at expiry.

• The settlement dates are different for these two indices. Stock options are often settled on the third Friday of the month with the settlement itself finalized on Saturday. With index options, the settlement date is the Thursdayjust before the third Friday of the month.

Capped index options

Index options can be capped. Capped index options are basically index options that are exercised automatically when a certain price is reached. Ifthis does not happen and the cap is not attained, the capped index option is exercised upon expiry.

Amex will help calculate the value of the cap. This concept is useful to understand. Please note that the entire value of a call write can be wipedclean should the underlying index rise sharply. To avoid catastrophe, the investor should be willing to settle for a lower premium.

With most options, stocks are the underlying commodities. However, indices are also an underlying security with other options. Basically, equities have largely been the underlying commodity for the indexes but in reality, though, the options market is much larger and quite complex than is depicted here. Let us take a look at other types of options.

Debt options

Options can be based on bonds. There are actually two different types of debt options. These are the price-based options and the yield based options. Let us look at each one separately.

• Yield based options: These options are settled using cash. The settlement is based on the actual difference between the value of the underlying security and the exercise price.

• Price based options: Owners or investors in these options have the right to sell or buy a defined, underlying debt instrument. The settlement of this option is often in the form of cash or physical delivery. This will depend on exactly how the contract was written.

Trading

Debt options are often traded on options platforms, the common one is Amex. On Amex, the debt options traded are usually based on securities fromthe US Treasury such as bonds. In the US, only foreign currency options have significant importance, but bonds based on securities in other countries securities are very rare.

Foreign currency options

Options can also be based on foreign currencies. Such options give an investor the right to sell or buy a specific currency whose price is based onthe value of another currency. When the price of one currency is based on the value of another currency, then this price is referred to as the exchange rate.

For instance assume that the British pound, also known as the GBP, has a value that is equivalent to $2. This then shows the exchange rate of 1 GBP is equivalent to $2.0. It can also be said that the exchange rate of the dollar is 0.5 GBP.

From the above, we can note the following:

• Exchange rate can be defined as the exercise price of a given currency option.

• As an example, an investor is of the opinion that the GBP or British pound will rise in value against the US$. Now, the investor may choose to invest funds to purchase a pound call that has an exercise price of $2.05.

• On Amex options trading

platform, foreign currencies are frequently traded and most are dollar denominated.

- Such a trader is then able to purchase what is known as a cross rate foreign currency option. This foreign currency option can take a position such as how the Euro is expected to perform based on another foreign currency such as the Japanese Yen.

Options and taxes

If you trade in options and make a profit, then you may need to know how to treat this when the time for taxes comes around. Taxation is not straightforward and may differ depending on the underlying commodity and the investor's tax status.

Other factors you need to consider include:

- Is an option still open, has it expired or been exercised?

- Is it uncovered or covered?

- Does the option represent a short or long option?

Basically, long options and short options that have been exercised will yield profits and will result in capital gains.

It is possible to buy options contracts on exchange-traded funds as well ason regular stocks. Buying options on exchange-traded funds is not without risk. However, it can be a little more predictable than doing it for individual stocks. That is because you are simply betting on the direction of the stock market or the price of some major index rather than tracking the fortunes ofan individual company.

One of the most popular index funds that is used is called SPY, namely for the S&P 500.

For those who don't know, an

exchange-traded fund is basically a mutual fund that trades like a stock. Investment companies collect a large amount of money, and then they buy shares in multiple companies. So, in the case of SPY, the fund owns shares in all 500 companies on the index. A large amount of money has to be assembled to make those kinds of investments.

Try and imagine if you wanted to invest in every single company that belongs to the S&P 500 or the Dow Jones industrial average. That would be quite a daunting task and unless you are a billionaire, it might even be impossible. But you could imagine trying to buy shares in each individual stock. Let's stick with the S&P 500 as an example. That would mean that you would have to pick out the 500 companies and buy shares in each one of them. Chances are not good for you to get very far in this task.

And then you have to take into account that this is not a static list of companies. That is, it will be changing with time. Companies can be removed from the list and new ones added as up and coming corporations replace others.

Another factor to consider would be that you really would not know the best ways to distribute your money among the different stocks even if you had enough to invest in all 500 companies. Usually, investments are weighted so that performance can be improved, as the idea is to beat the market. For this reason, it would be difficult for you, as an individual, to determine how to get the most growth out of your investments.

Therefore, it makes sense to leave such a project to professionals who have a lot of money to invest. So far it sounds like I have made a great argument for a mutual fund. And I suppose that mutual funds do have their advantages. For starters, we know that such funds automatically give you a diverse portfolio. Also, a professional money manager would attempt to build a portfolio with a higher probability of success, there would be a possibility that his or her fund would actually perform better than the S&P 500 index itself.

This is in fact, what professional money managers try to attempt with these funds. Instead of putting equal investments in each of the S&P 500 companies, what they will do is put a little bit more money in high growth companies and a little bit less in companies that are stable or even in decline.

Of course, while mutual funds have their advantages for people that are planning for retirement and so forth, they might be boring for people who are inclined to be traders, rather than safety-oriented long-term investors. And there is a good reason for this.

One thing to note about mutual funds is that they don't trade on the stock market. They only trade once a day after the market close. Also, mutual fundsare well-known for having high expenses. In fact, in case you didn't know, the expenses associated with mutual funds are a bit notorious if they have loads.

Exchange-traded funds were developed with the idea of taking the advantages of mutual funds but without the disadvantages. So, the first major difference between an exchange-traded fund and a mutual fund is that the exchange-traded fund is traded actively on the stock market. This is a book about options of course, so we are not going to get into all of the details of why that matters. However, consider the following scenario. Exchange-traded funds trade just like a stock during the day.

So, if the S&P 500 index were going up strongly, you could check the price of the exchange-traded fund, and you may want to get in action. This way you could buy your shares there and then, or at the right moment as the case may be. But you cannot do this in quite the same way for a mutual fund.

You could go ahead and submit an order during the day, but your order won't execute until the mutual fund trades at the end of the day. That means you really cannot be sure what price you are going to get. In contrast, an investor buying shares in an exchange-traded fund knows the exact price, just like anyone buying stock live does.

The second major advantage for exchange-traded funds over mutual funds is that they have very low expenses in comparison. So, the cost of investing in an exchange-traded fund as compared to a mutual fund that tracks the same index is going to be a lot lower.

For these reasons, many exchange-traded funds have become very popular. This is an excellent way for people to invest with diversification. So rather than having to deal with some fancy mutual fund with a bunch of polished publications, that are supposed to make you feel good about all the fees they are charging you, you can simply sign-on to your brokerage accountand buy shares of an exchange-traded fund whenever you feel like it.

The popularity of these exchange-traded funds has had a big impact on options as well.

Chapter 3: Understanding Options

The big question is: how do you apply your skills to make money on the stock market? You need to see the patterns and setups as they appear. This is followed by a possible application method. Rules are created. Charts show patterns and the locations where the rules for determining entry and exit points should be applied.

Determine whether the congestion is a re-accumulation or re-distribution based on the last increase or break. Assume this until the congestion pattern tells you otherwise.

The Stop

We propose two steps: an average spread below the last reaction low or the span of the entry bar below the entry bar. Once we have some freedom of movement, the stop will be tightened.

Close the position if the price does not behave within three bars. Then do not wait until the stop is triggered.

Trade or Not?

You do not risk your capital if you are not invested in the market. This trading style limits exposure to approximately 10% to 15% of the total observation period. Between 85% and 90% of the time, you are not in the market. During an accumulation or distribution phase, a position can be held. Although there is nothing wrong with this approach, it involves the risk of losing significant portions of the profits. The pattern may be distribution rather than accumulation. You need to study many charts until you find that this approach is workable and fits your trading style. This approach requires alot of judgment. They should try to automate as many rules as possible to minimize uncertainty.

Trade High-Value Assets

Active trading is best suited for the stocks and/or futures that are moving or in trend phases, and not the boring ones like the securities that are constantly going sideways. The definition of a value that moves is quite subjective. Many sources cite lists of securities that outperform and outperform others, and one of the best is Investor's Business Daily.

Moving securities may have the following characteristics:

• Increased volatility

• Reaching a new four-week high

• Securities in the rising phase

• Significantly upwards or downwards inclined sliding average of the last 20 days

- The leading values in a specific market segment

Brief Summary

Remember, the goal of this game is to win, not that you're in 90% of all price moves. Open your positions when certain patterns occur and realizeyour profits when the target price is reached or at the first sign that the offer exceeds demand.

These basic principles apply to every time horizon, including day trading. If you are long-term oriented, use weekly charts. This will lead to many false signals, but there are indeed the stops. You will only earn money by studying countless charts and drawing your entry points, exit points, and stop loss. Thereby you internalize these approaches and make them suitable. After that, you could succeed in trading. One of the hardest things in trading is closing a position towards the end of an outbreak or during a buying spike. Just tell yourself that you are a nice person: everyone wants to have the stock, and you give yours.

The General Motors study might be one example of how you can create a supply-demand based trade system. Create two charts: one shows what you should have done and the other what you did. Learn by comparison. Recognize the forces that act at important turning points.

Practical Application of the Elliott Wave Theory

The Elliott Wave Theory confuses many traders. We do not want to discuss the ambiguity of this theory, but we apply it to a trading plan that should develop into a successful approach. This theory is one of the best theories of the Cycle because it allows non-harmonic movements.

There are many different approaches to securities trading. These areroughly divided into fundamental and technical approaches. Some technicians like to mix both methods for an optimal market approach. The fundamental access includes bushels, hectares, consumption units, revenues, book values, and so on. Technical Analysis examines past price movements and predicts future ones. In 1939, Elliott published a series of articles describing the principle of Elliott waves. The Elliott Wave Theory is one of the best technical methods for market analysis, and the serious interest shouldcertainly include it in his studies.

Is it possible to predict price trends using the Elliott Wave Theory and use this information profitably? The answer to that is a cautious yes if you do not make the theory an exact science. The Elliott Wave Theory allows harmonic and non-harmonic course movements. Most cycle theories use principlesbased on harmonic movements. As soon as nonharmonic movements occur, it becomes difficult.

The following summary of the Elliott Wave Theory reduces the ideas to auseful size:

1.Ascending moves consist of five waves, two of which are corrections. Falling movements are counterproductive. The odd waves run in the direction of the main motion. Straight waves run against the main direction. Shaft 2 corrects shaft 1. Shaft 5 corrects shaft 4. Sometimes there are nine or more waves. Elliott solves this problem by calling these movement extensions.

2.The endpoint of shaft 4 is higher

than the height of shaft 1. Elliott specifies lengths proportions exactly, such as that the shaft 4 should beshorter than the waves 3 and 5. However, it has been found that this is not necessarily true.

The movements are divided into waves that are one degree smaller. What does "one degree smaller" mean? This question is difficult to answer, and thatis one of the reasons why applying the theory is so difficult. One suggestionis to look for it in the next shorter timeframe. If you have a daily chart, look for the smaller grade on a 30-minute chart. The next smaller degree also needs five waves to complete the higher-order wave 1 and is therefore identical to the daily chart.

Triangular Corrections

Triangular corrections consist of a five-point pattern (ABCDE) after a thrust. The type and position of such a pattern often allow conclusions to be drawn as to whether a turnaround is pending or not.

A-Shaped Corrections

The length and duration of the first correction wave or A-shaped correction of the thrust are of utmost importance for determining the further course of the total correction and the probability of a turnaround.

Look for the application of the A-wave (the first correction wave to increase) to determine the type of correction and the probable direction of the price after the correction has been completed. Then, you can see four possibleprice movements. If the extent of the A correction wave is the same, the following should be deduced:

- 25% - 35%: Indicates a single correction wave.

- 35% - 50%: Indicates a three-wave correction.

- 50% - 75%: Indicates a five-wave correction.

- Over 75%: mostly a possible trend reversal.

Prediction of the Corrections

This type of price development can lead to a turnaround. Here are the forces of supply and demand at work. A reaction at a distance of 75% from the starting point makes a clearer statement than a low-25% reaction.

Understanding Options Terminology

For logical reasons, the option's duration is a factor. If you'll like an asset to be controlled for five years rather than one year, normally, having it controlled for a longer period would cost more. Alternately, it would not cost as much, if you need the asset controlled for just one day,

This is because the more the asset is being controlled, the more likely it isthat something can happen (there's that word again) to affect its price. If for example, the property was controlled for just one day, it isn't too likely that amajor real estate bargain involving your property will be reported that day.

Chapter 4: Call Options, Put Options

There is a wide range of types and styles of options accessible. This segment gives a picture of each kind just as some essential wording each option investors ought to be comfortable with.

Call Options

A call option gives the investor the right (not the commitment) to buy the fundamental stock, security, item, or other instruments, at a particular cost within the time of the contract. The predefined cost is known as the strike cost. A speculator who is bullish on the stock, which means he anticipates that the stock should go up within a short time or inside the particular time span, would buy a call option.

For instance, say Investor A thinks stock XYZ is going to post high income one month from now, and the stock will go higher. So, she buys a calloption on the stock for \$20. The option agreement determines that she canbuy 100 portions of XYZ at a strike cost of \$100 inside the following 60days. If the cost of the stock falls beneath \$100, then she won't practice the option. The agreement will terminate uselessly and she will have lost the \$20 price tag. In any case, if the cost of the stock transcends \$100, state to \$130, then she will practice the option, buy the stock for \$100, and afterward, sell itat the higher market cost. She has now made a pleasant benefit.

The image below compares the payoff at maturity (in black) with the theoretical payoff of a long call position. The difference between the two values is due to the effect of 30 days the time value -as an example- on the option value (in gray).

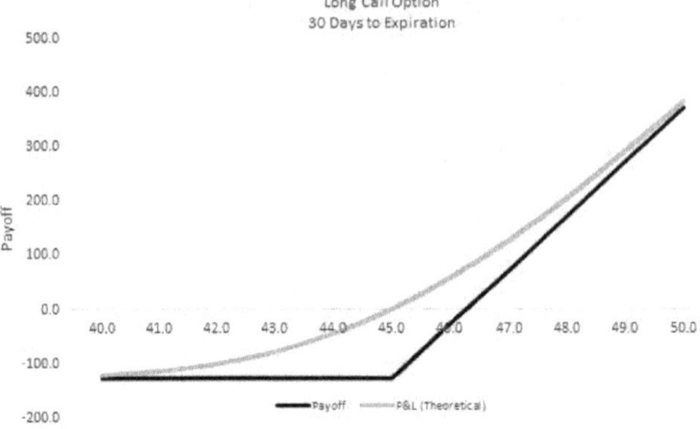

Put Options

A put option is something contrary to a call option. It gives the owner the right (however not the commitment) to sell the fundamental stock at a predetermined value (the strike cost) inside the predefined time span. An investor who is bearish on the stock, which means he thinks the stock cost is going down, would buy a put option.

For instance, say Investor B thinks stock XYZ is overrated and will decrease in cost throughout the following 60 days. He buys a put option on the stock for $20. The agreement gives him the option to sell the stock for

$120 inside the following 60 days. If the stock transcends $120 per share, then he would not practice the option. It would lapse useless, and he has lost his underlying speculation. If rather the cost of the stock dips under $120, to state $90, then he would practice his entitlement to sell the offers at $120 and pocket the distinction as a profit.

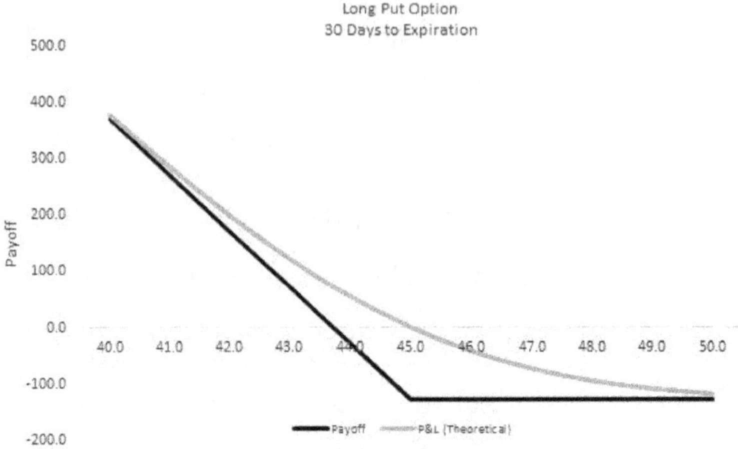

Using Call and Put Options to Make a Profit

There are various ways you can use call and put options. For instance, assume you believe that portions of US banks that are as of now selling for $200 per share are undervalued and will go higher in the following couple of months. You need more money to buy at least 100 portions of stock, yet might, in any case, want to bring in money from the ascent in the stock. For this situation, you could buy a call option on the stock, which would cost just a small amount of the cost of the stock. So, you buy the call option, and you presently reserve the option to buy 100 portions of the stock at $200 whenever in the following 60 days.

You may be thinking, how am I going to buy the stock in the next 60 daysfor $200 per share if I don't have the money? The appropriate response is that you don't really need to buy the stock to make a profit. If your impulses are right and the stock cost rises above $200, then your call option will turn outto be increasingly important. At the end of the day, as the stock value rises, the value of your option agreement likewise rises. You will have the option to sell the option agreement itself, rather than the stock, and make a benefit. Thehigher the value rises, the more your agreement will be worth.

Details of a payoff of a long call

position on MSFT share -as an example-.

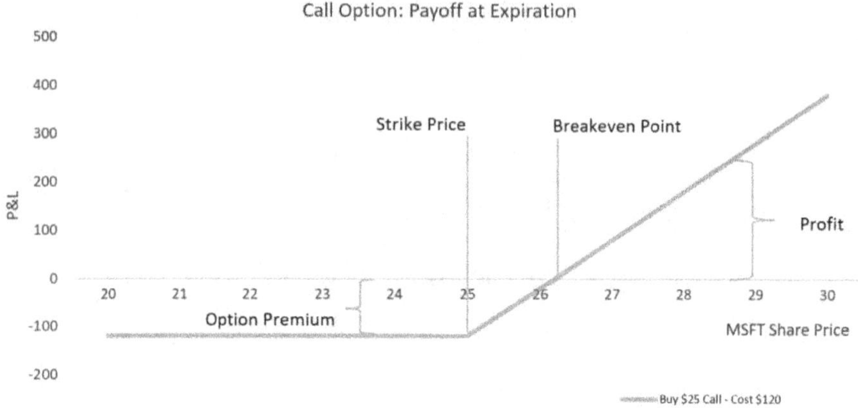

This works a similar route for a put option, but in this situation, you need the stock cost to fall. As the cost of the hidden security drops, the value of your put option will rise. The further the value falls, the more important is your option.

As should be obvious, by buying options, you can make a profit whether or not the stock is going up or down in cost.

Styles of Options

The past segments have given a review of the two essential sorts of options, calls, and puts. This segment will assist you in understanding the different styles of options accessible.

Most options that you will buy will can be categorized as one of two classifications, American or European. These are once in a while known as vanilla options. The principle distinction between the two is the point at which you can practice the option.

American Options

American options can be practiced whenever before the expiry date. Most options on stocks and value are of this sort. These are additionally the kind of agreements exchanged on fates trades.

European Options

European options must be practiced on the lapse date characterized in the agreement. These sorts of options are, for the most part, exchanged over-the-counter (OTC) advertise.

The values of the two option styles are determined marginally distinctively, and their termination dates are additionally unique. American options lapse the third Saturday of the month, while European options terminate the Friday before the third Saturday of the month.

Similitudes between the two incorporate the result and the strike cost. Theresult, either for calls or puts, is determined similarly for the two kinds. Inlike manner, the strike costs ordinarily are the equivalent.

Extraordinary Options

While the over two styles are the

primary ones most investors will manage, there is an assortment of increasingly colorful option sorts to know about too.

Bermuda Options

Bermuda options are in the middle of American and European options. In this kind of option, you are permitted to practice them on numerous dates during the agreement time frame.

Barrier Options

Barrier options are not the same as different sorts talked about so far in that all together for the option to result in the cost of the basic security must cross a specific level. They can be either be put or call options. There are foursorts of barrier options, which are plot beneath:

*Down-and-Out Barrier Options: A Down-and-Out Barrier Option gives the holder the privilege however not the commitment to buy (on account of a call) or sell (on account of a put) portions of a hidden resource at a foreordained strike cost since the cost of that advantage didn't go beneath a foreordained barrier during the option lifetime. That is, when the cost of the hidden resource falls underneath the barrier, the option is "took out" and no longer conveys any worth. Henceforth the name out for the count.

*Down-and-In Barrier Options: A down-and-in option is something contrary to a done for barrier option. Down-and-in options possibly convey value if the cost of the fundamental resource falls beneath the barrier during the options lifetime. If the barrier is crossed, the holder of the down-and-in option has the option to buy (if it is a call) or sell (if it is a put) portions of the hidden resource at the foreordained strike cost on the termination date.

*Up-and-Out Barrier Options: An up-and-out barrier option is like a done for barrier option, the main contrast being the arrangement of the barrier. Instead of being taken out by falling beneath the barrier cost, up-and-out options are taken out if the cost of the hidden resource transcends the foreordained barrier.

*Up-and-In Barrier Options: An up-and-in barrier option is like a down- and-in option; anyway, the barrier is set over the present cost of the hidden resource, and the option might be substantial if the cost of the basic resource arrives at the barrier before lapse.

Basket Options

A basket option, otherwise called a rainbow option, is an agreementwherein the worth depends on at least two basic resources. The option to practice the option is reliant on the costs of every fundamental resource.

Capped Style Options

In this kind of agreement, the most extreme benefit is set up. Capped options contain an arrangement where the option is practiced consequently if the fundamental security arrives at a specific set up cost. These kinds of options offer the author of the option a most extreme sum that can be lost.

Compound Options

These are fundamentally options to buy an option. Additionally, called split-expense options on the grounds that the holder must compensation two premiums, one forthright and one if the option is worked out.

Look back Options

This style of option supplies the holder the option to either buy or sell the fundamental security at its top (on account of calls) or most reduced (on account of puts), cost over a predetermined time span.

Asian Options

Asian options, otherwise called normal options, are those where the result is dependent upon the mean (normal) cost of the fundamental security over a particular period of time.

Binary Options

Binary options have a payout that is either a fixed sum or nothing by any stretch of the imagination. There are two sorts: money or-nothing and resource or-nothing. In the primary kind, the holder would get a fixed measure of money if the option lapses in-the-money. In the advantage or- nothing assortment, the holder would get the value of the hidden security. Otherwise called digital options, win big or bust options and fixed bring options back.

The bit of leeway to this kind of option is that the potential return is a known sureness before the option is bought. Notwithstanding, once bought, they can't be sold before the lapse.

Forward Start Options

Forward beginning options start with a vague strike value that will be resolved later on.

LEAPS

LEAPS represent Long-term Equity Anticipation Securities. LEAPS are basically equivalent to customary options with the exception of the more drawn out lapse dates. A LEAP can have a lapse date that is as long as three years away. The favorable position to this kind of option is there is much more opportunity for the basic stock, and along these lines option, to move toward the path you need it to.

Index Options

Notwithstanding buying options on singular protections, you can likewisebuy options on a stock list. These can be engaging even though they give an introduction to a whole gathering of stocks. List options are adaptable and can fit into the systems of both moderate and theoretical investors, during both a bull and a bear showcase. Most file options are European style options

Chapter 5: Buy and Selling Options

Now, we shall look at the mechanics of options trading, how to open a position, and how you can then close your employment opportunity if you want to. We will also look at how you sell options and the margin requirements that are connected to offering options.

We go over the new documents requirements you require to finish to trade options with your broker and how this may impact the option strategies your broker will permit you to carry out with them. Our last subject is the makers of the market. We discuss what they do and who they are.

Opening a position

You need to define or select the four essential regards to your option before you can sell an option or buy. The four basic terms (strike rate, the expiration date, the underlying stock, and if you are trading a put option or a call option) is set by the exchange. For underlying each commodity, therewill be a series of a variety of put and call options offered that have numerous strike costs and expiration dates. A list of the complete options is provided from the exchange and also from many brokers.

It is referred to as trade opening. Whenever you enter an options trade by either purchasing or selling an option. If you offered an option, it is a first sale, and if you bought an option, it is an opening purchase. Your option position, either as a seller or a purchaser, is described as an employment opportunity.

The overall variety of open contracts in a specific type of option is described as the interest open. The options by their code are listed, with a bid rate and an asking price. The bid cost is the cost at which someone wants to purchase this specific option, and the asking price is the cost at which somebody is willing to offer the option.

If you wish to purchase an option, you will put your order through your broker, just as you would buy a share. If you want to sell an option, you would likewise place your sale order through your broker.

You are able to place market and limit orders both for options. A market order is an order to sell or purchase at the best cost currently readily available on the market. A limit order is an order to sell or buy at a specific price only. You might wish to continue to hold that position if you currently have an open area that is nearing its expiry date. It is possible to use a mix order to execute both of these trades in a single order. You can define the net cost at which you want to roll over your position, but you do not require to determine a cost for the leg of each trade. If the order goes through, the close of both the preliminary position and the opening of a new location will be carried out at the same time.

It is vital to note options orders all on the ASX are suitable for day orders. This means that any requests that have not been filled at the end of thetrading day will be erased. If you still want to put your order the next day,you will require to place a new order in the early morning.

Closing a position

To close your option position, you just place an order to cancel out your employment opportunity. To narrow your option position, you would put an order to sell the same type and amount of the option contract if you had acquired an option.

Clearing Options

The clearing and settlement functions for the options market are entirely various from the market share. On the market share, all the trades are executed between a specific buyer and seller, and settlement of the business takes place three trading days later on. In Australia, the ASX does the functions of both solutions and trades.

Trading of Options on the ASX; however, a separate organization, ASX Clear, is accountable for the settlement function. This needs ASX Clear to both clear all options that are traded on the ASX and ensure that all contractual responsibilities associating with options are met. If an option holder wants to exercise their option, ASX Clear is accountable for ensuring that they designate this to an option seller and that the seller satisfies this obligation.

When you position an option order through your broker, your broker becomes your trading participant and is accountable for registering your trade with the ASX. When the trade is carried out, a contract is produced between your broker and the other celebration's broker. This contract is called the marketplace contract. At this point, a procedure of novation occurs in which the market agreement is changed by two separate agreements are as followed.

- Between the broker and ASX contract Clear

- A contract between the other celebration's broker and ASX Clear.

Under this procedure of novation, ASX Clear becomes the counterpartyto all open option positions. As an option buyer, you do not require toevaluate the credit danger of the seller and their capability to satisfy their commitments if you decide to work out or sell your option.

Purchasing or selling an option develops an agreement between parties. Unlike when you are buying or offer shares, there is no transfer of ownership or title to the underlying shares.

Option settlement

As we have simply described, ASX Clear is accountable for the settlement of all OPTION contracts. Solution for options agreements occurs one service day after the trade date. This is typically described as T +1 (where T stands for transaction day). This is different from share deals, whichpick the 3rd service day after the agreement and are referred to as T +3.

You need to pay your premium one service day after you purchase it if you buy an options contract. You will receive the incentive of one business day after you have sold it if you offer an option.

Exercise options

If you exercise or wish to buy your option, you require to notify your broker who is required to send a workout notice to ASX Clear. When ASX Clear receives a workout notice, it will arbitrarily choose an author who has sold the same type of OPTION and will designate the workout to the writer.It is far too late to liquidate your position as soon as ASX Clear has assigneda workout notice to an option you have offered.

When an option is worked out, the transaction is settled within three working days after the option is exercised; that is, T +3. This is in line with the stocks of settlement. This is a reason that the option's writer can purchase the underlying stock from the marketplace (which settles T 3) if they require to adhere to the workout of a call option, and they do not presently hold that stock. You will receive and pay for the underlying shares three service days after exercise if you exercise your call option. If you have offered a call option that is applied, you will receive payment for the shares at the strike rate and need to deliver the shares three service days after the exercise.Option agreements are settled T +1.

The workout of options are settled T +3. If you exercise or do not an in-the-money OPTION before the expiry date, it will end worthless, despite just how much intrinsic value might be attached to that options. To prevent this, you need to guarantee that you monitor your option positions and either offer or exercise your options before the date of expiry.

It is possible to set account for trading to auto-exercise so that your options will automatically be exercised if they are in-the-money at expiry. This is particularly helpful for cash-settled index options, as the workout of the options continually leads to a cash payment rather than the delivery of an underlying share.

Trading expenses

Payable Brokerage will be on any OPTION orders that are carried out. Brokerage rates will differ in between brokers and might be payable at a flat rate or as a percentage based upon the option premium, or a mix of both a flat rate and a portion. You will need to consult private brokers to identify the brokerage rates and structure that will best suit you. ASX Clear likewise charges a cost per contract, which may be included in your brokerage or may be charged to you separately by your broker. You will also pay an exercisefee if you want to exercise your OPTION.

Limits

When you write a contract of an OPTION, you have a prospective obligation to deliver the underlying shares if that OPTION is worked out. As an OPTION author, you may likewise have potentially limitless danger if the market moves versus your position. To ensure you can fulfill this obligation, ASX Clear requires all options writers to provide a margin.

Tip

If you offer an options agreement, you only need to supply a margin. Option buyers need not provide any margin for their employment opportunities.

ASX Clear determines the quantity of a security that it deems needed to ensure that the option's writer can meet their obligations under the options contract. As the options agreement worth is impacted by the market price of the underlying stock, the value of any margin requirement will also change as the market price of the underlying stock changes.

ASX Clear computes the margin requirements utilizing a system referred to as the ASX Margining DERIVATIVE System (ADMS). This marginal calculation of requirement using a set formula that considers the current option premium and the volatility of the hidden security. The margin needed for options consists of two parts:

•A margin premium

•The risk margin

The margin is the premium value of the premium connected to your OPTION at the close of every day. This is generally the quantity you would need to close out your option position by buying the same type of options.

The risk margin is developed to cover the possible motion in the premiummargin on any given day. This is determined by the recommendation to the intraday movement of the price of the hidden share, and this movement is referred to as the daily volatility. This volatility is expressed as a portion and understood as the margin period. The ASX publishes and updates the margin for all OPTION classes each week.

Your margin requirement will be computed on your whole portfolio of open options agreements so that some positions might offset the marginrequirements of other positions every day.

As you understand, because of the procedure of novation. ASX Clear has a broker contract with your option agreement, instead of with you straight. ASX Clear will enforce the margin on your broker, who will, in turn, require you to offer them with a margin for your option contract. You must know that your broker might examine your margin threat differently to ASX Clear and need a more significant margin than that calculated under ADMS.

Chapter 6: Financial Leverage in Options

Leverage is a concept that is used by both companies and investors. For investors, the notion of leverage is used to try and increase returns that come on investment. To use leverage, you have to make use of various instruments, including future, options, and margin accounts.

The use of leverage in options trading helps boost your profits. Trading inoptions can give you huge leverage and allow you to generate huge profits from a small investment.

Definition

Leverage is the ability to trade a large number of options using just a small amount of capital. Many traders feel that leverage is riskier then "normal" trading, but studies have found that the risk in leveraged options is nearly the same to non-leveraged securities.

Why Is Leverage Riskier?

Trading options using leverage is usually considered riskier because it exaggerates the potential of the business. For instance, you can use $500 to enter a trade that has a potential of $7000. Remember the first rule of trading
– don't trade what you cannot lose.

This isn't as true as it seems, which is why it is vital that you know what you are doing at all times.

Leverage makes you utilize capital more efficiently. For this reason,many traders love the trade because it allows them to go for larger positions with limited capital.

When you use leverage, you don't reduce the potential profit that you will gain; rather, you reduce the risk in certain trades. For instance, if you want to put your money in 10,000 options at $8 per share, you would need to risk $80,000 worth of investment. This means that the whole amount of $80,000 would be at risk. However, you can use leverage to place a smaller amount of money, thus reducing the risk of loss.

This is the way you need to look at leverage, which is the right way.

Before you can trade leverage, you need to find a way to maximize the gains in each trade. Here are a few tips that you can explore:

Know When to Run

You need to cut losses early enough and then let your winning trades run to completion. Just the way you run other trades; you need to know when to cut your losses so that you don't end up bankrupt. You need to make use of stop losses when running leverage in trades.

Have a Stop Loss Set

As a trader, you need to determine your stop loss set so that you don'tlose more than you can afford. The set that you come up with will depend upon the situation of the market at any time. Whatever the case, always makesure you have a set to guide you.

Don't Go with the Trade

Many traders try to chase a trade to the finish, something that ends up discouraging them and making them lose money. Once a move happens, you need to accept and wait for the next opening. Always be patient because just like the other opportunity came along, another one will definitely come by.

Have Limit Orders

Instead of placing market limits, opt for limit orders instead so that you can save on fees. The limit orders also help you reign in your emotions when you trade.

Learn About Technical Analysis

Make sure you learn about technical analysis before you jump into trading. Technical analysis will make sure you have the information that you need to make decisions fast.

The Advantages of Leverage in Options Trading

When you use leverage, you increase your financial capability as a trader and enjoy better trading results. You can change the amount of leverage at your discretion. This is because when you open a trading account, you have all the power of managing the amount of capital that you place on a trade. The good news is that you can use leverage free of charge, but you need to make sure you know how it works and whether it will work for you or not.

The level of leverage varies. Some trading platforms offer leverage from as low as 1:1 up to and beyond 1:1000. As a trader, it is advisable that you gofor the largest leverage possible so that you can make the biggest returns.

Another advantage is that low leverage allows you as a new trader to survive. When starting out in options trading, you have the capacity to make small trades with little to show for your efforts. With leverage, you can make use of leverage to place trades that run into thousands of dollars without risking the same amount in terms of investment. As long as you know what you are doing, you have the capability to enjoy massive profits.

Disadvantages of Leverage in Options Trading

As much as it is a good way to make huge profits, you also need to understand that leverage comes with many demerits. These include:

Magnifies the Losses

With leverage, you will be faced with huge losses if the trade decides to go the other way. And since the original outlay is way smaller than what you end up losing, many traders forget that they are placing their capital at risk. Make sure you come up with a ratio that will help protect your interests and then know how to manage trade risk.

No Privileges

When you use leverage to trade, you

sacrifice full ownership of the asset. For instance, when you use leverage, you give up the opportunity of enjoying dividends. This is because the amount on the dividend is deducted from the account regardless of the position of the trade.

Margin Calls

A margin call is when the lender asks you to add funds so that you keep the trade open. You have to decide whether you wish to add funds or exit a position to reduce the exposure.

Incur Expenses

When you use leverage to trade options, you will receive the money from the lender so that you can use the full position. Most traders opt to keep their positions open overnight, which attracts a fee to cover the costs.

Choosing the Right Leverage

You need to look at different factors

when choosing the kind of leverage that will work for you.

First, you need to start with low levels of leverage, because the more you

borrow, the more you will need to pay back. Second, you need to use stops to make sure you protect the amount you have borrowed. Remember losses won't go down well with you.

All in all, you need to choose leverage which you find is comfortable for you. If you are a beginner, go for low leverage so that you minimize risks. If you know what you are doing, then go for maximum leverage to build your returns.

Using stops on order allows you to reduce loses when the trade changes direction. As a newbie, this is the only protection you need to make it in the market. This is because you will learn about the trades and how to place them while limiting any losses that might arise.

How to Manage Risk in Options Trading

Options trading comes with a number of risks that you need to manage so that you can enjoy the profits and minimize losses.

Here are a few risks and how to deal with them.

Losing More than What You Have

This risk is inherent in options trading, especially if you are using leverage to make a trade. It means that you put up a small fraction of the initial deposit to open the trade. This means that your fate is in the hands of the direction of the market. If it goes along with your prediction, you willgain more than the deposit. On the other hand, if the direction changes and you lose the position, you might end up losing more than your initial deposit.

When this happens, you need to have a strategy in place to help mitigate the risk. What you need to do in this case is to set a limit, so that you define the exact level at which the trade should stop so that you don't lose more thanyou can handle.

Positions Closing Unexpectedly

When positions close unexpectedly, they lead to loss of money. To keep the trades open, you need to have some money in the account. This aspect is called the margin, and if you don't have enough funds to cover the margin, then the position might close.

To mitigate this, you need to keep an eye on the running balances and always add funds as needed.

Sudden Huge Losses or Gains

The market can turn out to be volatile, and when it does, you need to move fast. Markets change depending on the news or something else in the market, which can be an announcement, event, or changes in trader behavior.

Apart from having stops, you also need to get notifications regarding any upcoming movement, which tells you whether to react or not.

Orders Filled in Erroneously

When you give instructions to a broker to place a trade for you, and the broker instead does the opposite. This is termed slippage. When this happens,use guaranteed stops to make sure you protect yourself against any slippage that might occur.

How to Trade Smarter Using Leverage

Even with leverage in tow, you need to have a way to trade better. With many mistakes occurring during a trade, you stand to lose more than gain if you don't have the right tips to excel. Let us look at the top mistakes that you go through to get to the top.

You need to make sure you try out a few new strategies depending on the level of trading you want to achieve. Most traders get a single strategy and then stick to it even when it is not working out for them. When this happens, you are often tempted to go against the rules that you set down.

Maintain an open mind so that you can learn new option trading strategiesto help you get more out of your trades.

Chapter 7: Strike Price

The strike price is one of the most important if not the most important thing to understand when it comes to option contracts. The strike price will determine whether the underlying stock is actually bought or sold at or beforethe expiration date. When evaluating any options contract, the strike price is the first thing that you should look at. It's worth reviewing the concept and how it's utilized in the actual marketplace.

The strike price will allow you to reach the profits that can be made on an options contract. It's the break-even point but also gives you an idea as to your profits and losses. Of course, the seller always gets the premium no matter what.

For a call contract, the strike price is the price that must be exceeded by the current market price of the underlying equity. For example, if the strike price is $100 on a call contract, and the current market price goes to any price above $100, then the purchaser of the call can exercise their right at any time to buy the stock. Then the stock can be disposed of with a profit. Suppose that the current price rises to $130. Then you can exercise your option to buy the stock at $100 a share, and then turn around and sell it on the market for $130 a share, making a $30 profit per share before taking into account the premium and other fees that might accrue with your trades. While as the buyer of the contract you have no obligations other than paying the premium,the seller must sell you the shares at $100 per share no matter how much it pains them to see the $130 per share price.

For a put contract, the strike price likewise plays a central role, but the value of the stock relative to the strike price works in the opposite way. A putis a bet that the underlying equity will decrease in value by a certain amount. Hence if the stock price drops below the strike price, then the buyer can exercise their right to sell the shares at the strike price even though the marketprice is lower. So, if your price is $100, if the current price of the equitydrops to $80, the seller obligated to buy the 100 shares per contract from you at $100 a share even though the market price is $80 per share. In this case, you've made a gross profit of $20 a share.

The value of the strike price will not only tell you profitability but give you an indication of how much the stock must move before you are able to exercise your rights. Often when the amount is smaller, you might be better off. When you know the strike price of different options contracts, then you can evaluate which one is better for you to buy. Suppose that a stock is currently trading at $80 and you find two options put contracts. One has a strike price of $75 and the other has a strike price of $60. Further, let's suppose that both contracts expire at the same time. In the first case, the stockprice in the market will need to drop just $5 before the contract becomes profitable. For the second contract, it will have to drop $20.

The potential worth of each contract per share is the difference. For the contract with the $75 strike price, that is only $5. For the second contractwith the strike price of $60, the potential worth is $20, four times as much.

Determining which contract is better is a matter of analysis and taking some risk. You can't just go by face value, but you must take into consideration the expiration date together with an analysis of what the stock will actually do over that time period. It may be that it's going to be impossible for the stock to drop $20 in order to make the second contract valuable. If the expiration date comes before the stock drops that much in price, the contract will be worthless. In other words, you'd never be able to exercise your option of selling shares at strike amount. On the other hand, even though there is not much discrepancy between the strike and the market amount for the first contract, and the market price might only drop to say $70 per share, the chances of this happening before the expiration date is more likely.

Your analysis might be different if the contract with the lower strike price has a longer expiration date.

The lesson to take to heart is that

a stock is more likely to move by smaller amounts over short time periods. But the higher the risk, the more thepotential profits.

Chapter 8: Moneyness

The concept of moneyness is an easy concept to explain in options trading.

It is one of the fundamentals of options trading, and you must be conversant with it.

When you hear options traders using the term "moneyness," he or she refers to the relationship that exists between the predetermined price (strike) and the current price of the stock.

I will describe the three main terms used in describing the concept of moneyness in options trading. These terms include in-the-money, at-the-money, and out-of-the-money. There is also a fourth term, near-the-money.

Finally, you will understand the importance of the concept of moneyness in Options Trading. Let's explain these concepts.

Out of the Money

You consider an option to be "out-of-the-money" in options trading when the option does not have intrinsic value.

Meanwhile, a put option will be out-of-the-money if the predetermined price is lower or below the stock price.

Alternatively, out-of-the-money is a situation where the underlying asset or security is trading at a price that does not favor the buyer of the options.

Remember in the first part, I indicated that an option price comprises of two components: intrinsic value and time value.

The intrinsic value deals with profits that exist in an option, whereas the time value is influenced by different factors, including expiration time, volatility, interest rate, the value of the underlying asset, and dividend.

Consider the out-of-the-money option for both the call and put options.

Call Options for Out of the Money

Price of Stock	Call Option	Intrinsic Value	Out of the Money
$100	$120	$0	Yes
$140	$80	$60	No
$150	$165	$0	Yes

Put Options for out of the Money

Price of Stock	Put Option	Intrinsic Value	Out of the Money
$100	$120	$20	No
$140	$80	$0	Yes
$150	$165	$15	No

Call option (intrinsic value = market stock price – predetermined price)

Put option (Intrinsic value = predetermined price – market stock price)

From the formula, can you understand how come about the various valuein the table? Of course, you should.

At the Money Options

You can say an option is "at-the-money" when the predetermined price is equal to the stock price.

Similar to the out-of-the-money concept of moneyness, it does not have intrinsic value. This concept is applicable to both the call and put options.

Furthermore, this concept is expensive than the preceding money option because the price of the stock has to move below in order to create intrinsic value.

Although the definition of the at the money options is when the predetermined price is equivalent to the price of the stock, it is rare to find such a situation since the stock price is ever changing.

Price of Stock	Call/Put Option	At the Money
$100	$140	No
$165	$165	Yes
$160	$170	No

The call option and put option are both different.

A call option in the money situation occurs when the stock price is higher than the predetermined price, whereas the put option occurs in a situation where the stock price is lower than the predetermined price.

They are the most expensive moneyness concept in options trading.

Additionally, many experts recommend this concept for beginners because it is easier to regulate risks if, by chance, they cost more.

Let us assume you own this option, and the expiry date is fast approaching, it is better to sell them because once it gets to the point of expiration, they are automatically exercised. This may not be what you want to see.

Call option of "in the money."

Price of Stock	Call Option	Intrinsic Value	in the Money
$100	$150	$0	No
$140	$80	$60	Yes
$150	$120	$30	Yes

From the call option above, you can see that when the call option price is below the price of the stock, it means it has intrinsic value.

Put Options of "in the Money"

Price of Stock	Put Option	Intrinsic Value	in the Money
$100	$120	$20	Yes
$140	$80	$0	No
$150	$165	$15	Yes

The table above shows that when the call option price is higher than the stock price, then it is in the money because the put option has intrinsic value. **Near the Money**

Although this moneyness concept isn't part of the three aforementioned standards, however, it is used commonly. It occurs when the predetermined price is close to the price of the stock or asset. This moneyness concept is either slightly between the out of the money or in the money options.

Importance of the Concept of Options Moneyness A fundamental understanding of the concept of options moneyness and its various states is quite simple for anyone to assimilate. They are common phrases used in options trading and are essential for you to be conversantwith them.

Irrespective of the options trading strategy you use, you need fundamental knowledge of moneyness state. Perhaps you are using a simple strategy that requires a single position, you still require the concept of option moneyness.

For instance, if you decide to buy a stock and anticipate that the price will move dramatically in a short period, then using the out of the money option will be the best option to maximize your profits. However, if you anticipate a little movement, then in the money option provides a better and less dicey investment.

Immediately you start using complex strategies in options trading; the concept of moneyness becomes important in your trading. Different advanced trading strategies require several positions on different options.

For these strategies to work effectively, it is crucial to trade options using the right moneyness concept. For instance, a particular strategy may require you buying an option and earlier selling out the option of the same stock.

If you lack the knowledge on the concept of moneyness, you will make the mistake of buying or selling the option in the wrong moneyness state. However, you can navigate through this situation if your knowledge of moneyness is well-polished to use the right trading strategies properly.

Hurry! You have the knowledge of the concept of moneyness. You arenot in the dark anymore whenever a trader talks about using moneyness. You can navigate your way through any situation you face in the market.

Risk Management

Trading is generally not without risk and options pose a higher riskcompared to other forms of securities. The risk is largely due to its speculative nature. As a trader, you need to protect yourself and trading capital from unnecessary losses and any potential losses that can be prevented.

As a trader, the first thing you need to think about is not losing money. We do not engage in trade in order to lose money. A lot of beginners lose money in their early days. Some believe that this is an inevitable process. However, it does not have to be this way. With proper planning and especially proper risk management, you should not unnecessarily lose money trading the markets.

In fact, to be successful as a trader, your number one focus should be risk management rather than winning trades or strategies. A good trader is one who does not unnecessarily lose money. The most successful traders arethose who manage their funds so well. To do this, you have to watch your every move and countercheck every decision that you make. For instance, if you want to enter a position in the markets, you need to ask yourself if thatmove is necessary and what amounts you stand to lose if it does not work out.

Chapter 9 :Volatility in Options Prices Dynamics

Trading on news requires some attention on your part. You are going to have to think ahead in order to implement this strategy and profit from it. Remember that you can use a straddle or strangle any time that you think the stock is going to make a major shift one way or the other. An example of a non-earning season situation, where this could be a useful strategy, would bea new product announcement. Think Apple. If Apple is having one of their big presentations, if the new phone that comes out disappoints the analysts, share prices are probably going to drop by a large amount. On the other hand,if it ends up surprising viewers with a lot of new features that make it the must-have phone again, this will send Apple stock soaring.

The problem here is you really don't know which way it's going to go. There are going to be leaks and rumors but basing your trading decisions on that is probably not a good approach, often, the rumors are wrong. A strangle or straddle allows you to avoid that kind of situation and make money either way.

Other situations that could make this useful include changes in management or any political interaction. We mentioned the government recently made a privacy settlement with Facebook. If you knew when the settlement was going to occur but wasn't sure what it was going to be, usinga strangle or straddle might be a good way to earn money from the large pricemoves that were sure to follow.

The same events that might warrant buying a long call such as a GDP number or jobs report, for options on index funds, are also appropriate for strangles and straddles.

Implied Volatility Strategy

Implied volatility is very important when a big event like an earnings report is coming. This gives you a way to make profits. In fact, we are going to call this the implied volatility strategy.

Let's review how this would work. Remember, implied volatility is a projection of what the volatility of the stock is going to be in the near future.

When there is an earnings call, the volatility is going to be extreme on the day after the call. Therefore, you are going to see the implied volatility growing as earnings day approaches.

At the time I am writing this, it is 24 hours before Facebook's earnings call.

The implied volatility is 74%, which is very high. In contrast, for Apple, which is more than a week away from its next earnings call, the implied volatility is only 34%. This is for a $207.50 strike put, with a share price of $207.9.

The strategy is to profit from the implied volatility. You want to enter your position one to two weeks before the earnings call or big announcement. As implied volatility increases, this is going to swamp out time decay and cause a big rise in the option price.

Using that Apple put option, if we assumed that there were only 4 days to expiration, but the implied volatility had risen to about where Facebook is and there were no other changes (so we will leave the share price where it was), the price of the put option would increase by about $330.

So, if nothing else, you could profit from the change of implied volatility. It will probably go highest the day before the earnings call.

This is going to be magnified if you trade a strangle or straddle. Prior to the earnings call, both the put and the call option are going to increase a greatdeal in value because of implied volatility. So, you could sell the strangle the day before the earnings call and book some profits then. Since a strangle or straddle can earn big profits if there is a large move in the share price, you won't find any problems locating a buyer.

Estimating Price from Implied Volatility

If you know the implied volatility, you can make an estimate of the price range of the stock. This can be done using a simple formula.

(Stock price x implied volatility)/SQRT (days in a year)

If you don't want to do the calculation, if we take the square root of 365,it is about 19.1. For example, we use Facebook with a share price of $202.50 and an implied volatility of 76%.

The implied volatility gives us an idea of what traders are thinking, in regard to the upcoming earnings call, but of course, we can never be sure what is really going to happen until it does. But this gives us upper and lower bounds. Using the information that we have available, we can guess that Facebook might rise to $210.56 a share after the earnings call, or it might drop to $194.44 per share after the earnings call. You can use these boundaries to set up your strategy. However, remember that if there is a big surprise, it can go well past these boundary points in one direction or the other.

What is a Long Straddle?

To set up a straddle, you buy a put option and a call option simultaneously (buy = take a long position). The maximum loss that you can incur is the sum of the cost to buy the call option plus the sum of the cost to buy the put option. This loss is incurred when you enter the trade.

With a straddle, you buy a call option and a put option together. And theywould be with the same strike price. By necessity, this means that one option is going to be in the money and one option is going to be out of the money. When approaching an earnings call, the prices can be kind of steep, because you want to price them close to the current share price. That way, it gives us some room to profit either way the stock price moves.

A maximum loss is only incurred if you hold the position to expiration. You can always choose to sell it early, if it looks like it's not going to work out and take a loss that is less than the maximum.

There is a total premium paid for entering into the position. This is the amount of cash paid for buying the call added to the money paid for buying the put. This is called the total premium. There are two breakeven points:

To the upside, the breakeven point is the strike price + total premiumpaid.

On the downside, the breakeven point is the strike price – total premium paid.

It the price of the stock moves up past the breakeven point, the put is worthless. However, the call option would earn substantial profits. On the other hand, if the stock price moved down past the lower price point, that would be the breakeven, the call option would be worthless and the putoption would earn substantial profits.

For example, suppose that we buy a $207.5 straddle on Apple 7 days to expiration with an implied volatility of 35%, and the underlying price is $207. The total cost to enter the position is $8.03 ($803 total). At 1 day to expiration, the share price breaks up to $220 a share after the earnings call. The put expires worthless, but the call jumps to $12.50. The net profit is then $12.50 - $8.03 = $4.47, or $447 in total per contract.

If instead, the share price had dropped to $190, the call expires worthless,and the put jumps to $17.50 per share. The net profit, in this case, is then $17.50 - $8.03 = $9.47 per share or a total of $947.

This isn't to say that the straddle would be more profitable for a stock decrease, it is not. The profit will be the same no matter which way the share price moves, in our examples, we used two different sized moves. The pointis to illustrate that no matter which direction the stock moves, you can profit.

If the stock is at the money at expiration, we could still recoup some ofthe investment and sell the straddle for a loss. In this case, the call and the put would both be priced at $152. We'd still be at a loss, but we could recoup $304 by selling both at $152.

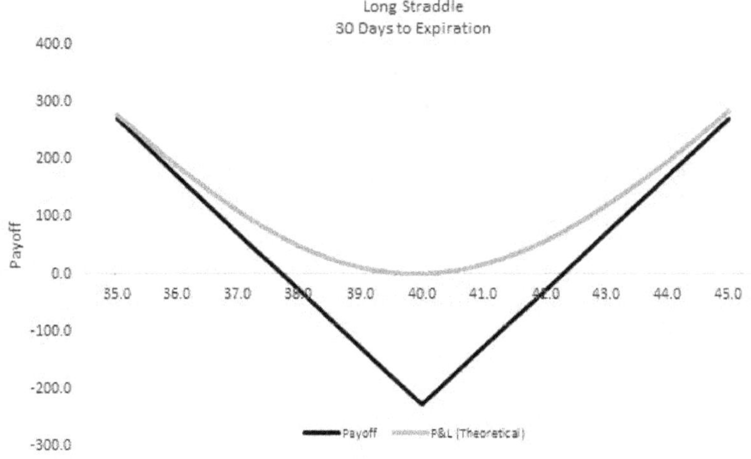

Short Straddle

If you sell a straddle, then you are taking the opposite position, which means you would be betting that the share price stays inside the range and hope that the stock didn't make a big move to the upside or the downside. To sell a straddle you'd have to either be able to do a covered call and protected put or be a level 4 trader who could sell naked options.

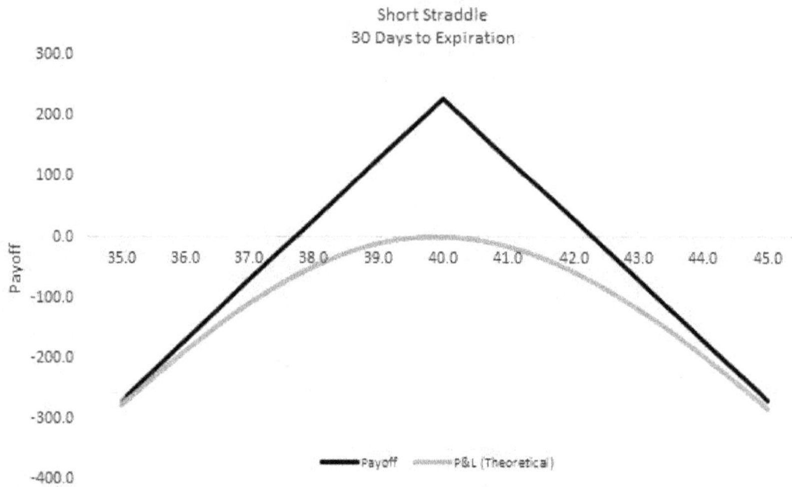

Long Strangle

A strangle is similar to a straddle, but in this case, the strike prices are different. In this case, you will buy a just barely out of the money call option, while simultaneously buying a slightly out of the money put option. The two options will have the same expiration date. The breakeven points for a strangle are going to be calculated in a similar way as the breakeven prices for a straddle, but you are going to use the individual strike prices for the call and put because they are different. So, you calculate the total premium paid, which is the total amount paid for the call option plus the premium paid for the put option. Then the breakeven points are given by the following formulas:

To the upside, the breakeven point is the strike price of the call + total premium paid.

On the downside, the breakeven point is the strike price of the put – total premium paid.

In a similar fashion as compared to a long straddle, the maximum loss is going to occur when the share price ends up in between the two strike prices. Therefore, you might want to choose strike prices that are relatively close, in order to minimize the range over which the loss can occur. Of course, there isa tradeoff here because the closer in range the strike prices are, the more expensive it is going to be in order to enter the position. But, it's going to increase your probability of profit because if the strike prices are tight about the current share price, there is a higher probability that the share prices are going to exceed the call strike + premium paid, or decrease below the put strike price less the price paid to enter the contract (the premium).

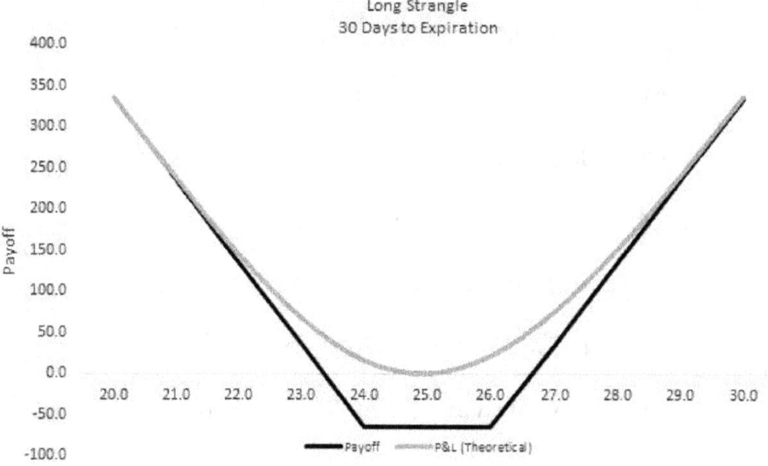

Chapter 10: Purchasingand Selling Options

Selling options is a lucrative income-generating process. It is not uncommon for traders to make 2%—2.5% returns each month. However, this is not the only pathway to riches in the markets. You can also sell naked puts. This is similar in a way to selling shares or stocks that you do not.

When you sell naked put options, you will free up your time so that you can do a lot more. Stock trading allows you an opportunity to sell stocks of shares that you do not have for a profit. This tends to free up your capital so you can invest it or trade with it indefinitely. It is advisable to stick to stocks that you understand very well and those that you would not mind ing. There is still hedging that is associated with options trading, so always be careful and watch about that. Most large investors who deal in options are often hedging.

This is the detail of the payoff of a short position of a call on a MSFT share -as an example-. As you can see the risk of loss in this case has nolimit.

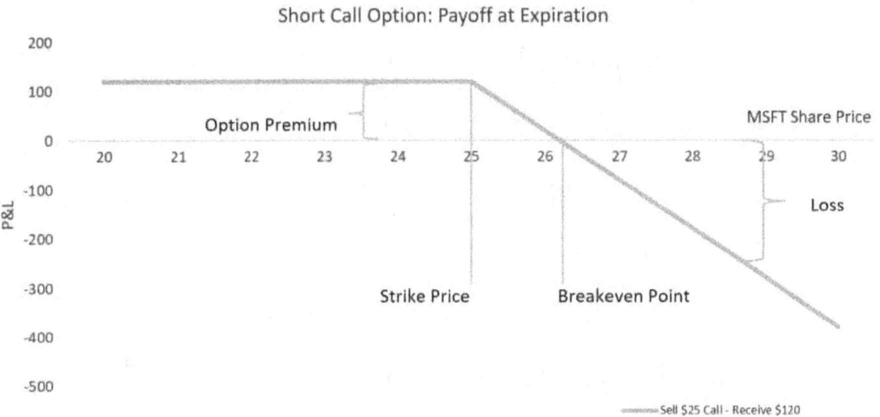

Options Trading and Leverage

One of the other larger applications of options trading is leveraging.Leverage allows you to manipulate situations in your favor. Let us use an example to illustrate this. Let us assume that an investor has about $1000 to trade. The investor desired to purchase options that will provide him with the best profit margin. He chooses to buy bullish ABC, Inc. shares.

ABC shares cost $100 apiece so he can afford to purchase only ten shares. Now, ABC also has several call options. These have a price of $105 and 3 months. Each option costs $3. Now instead of opting for the shares, our investor decides to purchase three call option contracts. They cost him $300. Shortly after that, the stock price moves to $130.

Now, if he had invested the money in the shares, he would have made a profit.

$100 * 10 = $1000

$130 * 10 = $1,300

Difference is $1,300—$1,000 = $300

Buying the shares outright brings in $300 only

Now, what if he had opted for options?

3 options at $3 per each is = $9

Profit for this trade is $9 * 100 * 3 = $2,700

$2,700—$900 (premium) = $1,600

It is evident to note that options trading is much more lucrative compared to a direct stock purchase. There is some risk associated with buying the options. Some of these include insufficient price movement and so on. There is also the risk of time decay where an option's time runs out.

Always Consider all the Options Available to You

A lot of the time, we make assumptions that traders will hold their positions till the end. However, this is not always the case, especially if you are trading American options. In this instance, you can choose from several options to ensure that you can leverage any time you want if you see the needfor it. In our situation above, our trader could have done any of the following.

- Sold off the option to lock in some profits

- Sell off the option before time runs out to just recoup losses

- Exercise the right to buy shares and then simply buy the shares

Learn to Select the Right Options to Trade

There are some guidelines that you need to learn and follow every time you want to acquire options. This way, you will be able to identify options that will see you earn a profit. Here is a look at the guidelines.

- Determine whether you are bullish or bearish on the market, sector, or just the stock. Also, make sure you determine whether you are strongly bullish or just a tiny bit bullish. When you make these decisions, then youwill be able to identify the kind of options that you wish to buy.

• Consider volatility and think about how it would affect your options trading strategy. Also, think about the status of the market. Is it calm, or is it volatile? If it is not very high, then you should be able to buy call options based on the underlying stock. These are normally quite cheap.

You may also want to consider the expiration date and strike price. If you only have a couple of shares, then this would be a great time and opportunity to purchase more stock.

Here are Some Options Trading Tips

• If you are purchasing options, you will aim to acquire those with the longest expiration dates. This way, you would be giving your trades sufficient time to work out. However, should you be writing options, then please tryand opt for the options offering the shortest time possible? This way, you will limit your liability.

● Also, when you buy your options as in the case above, remember to go for the cheapest of them all. Cheap options will likely help to improve your chances of making a profit. Such trades also have minimal volatility and also tend to perform well at the markets. When this trade works out, then the rewards will be huge. It is better to purchase options with low volatility ratherthan those with high. This will minimize the risk of losses should the tradenot work out.

● Always ensure that you understand as much as you can about the specific sector you will be trading. Take the biotech sector, for example. Trade-in these stocks often ends up with binary outcomes. This tends to happen mostly during announcements of clinical trials of an important type ofmedication. You can then find or choose out-of-the-money put options and call options.

• If you are to buy a deeply out-of-the-money call option, then it is much better to purchase stocks in the telecoms and energy firms. Such firms showcase very little volatility and are considered a safe bet. On the other hand, you can buy out-of-the-money options just before an earnings report is considered a profitable venture, especially if that stock had been d for awhile. In short, if you are a trader who prefers lower-risk options, then you should focus your energy on buying low volatility options. Options are generally profitable because there are many different paths you can follow to attain maximum profitability at low risk.

Chapter 11: Covered Calls,Protective Put

What is covered call strategy?

Covered call is a combination of stock and option positions. In particular, it is length of the calls sold shares on the stock, which "cover" position. Covered calls are bullish on the stock, and bearish volatility. A covered call option selling is the position of the net. This means you assume some risk in exchange for premium available on the options market. This "risk" is that your old stock will be taken of you with a call option is known as a risk buyer-- tasks.

A covered call is a strategy that involves the selection of the second trading in the underlying shares and options contracts. The purchase trader or an underlying stock or asset. They then sell the call option (right to buy the underlying assets, or stock it) and then wait for the option contract must be executed or ended. Covered Calls are a common strategy used to improve the long stock position. Position limits the potential benefits to long stock positions by selling a call option on the stock.

This is most often done with equities, but can be used for all securities and instruments that have a market options associated with them. For many traders, covered calls are luring investment strategy given that they provide close to equity like return, but usually with lower volatility. This is because even if the underlying price contradict you, call option will be flowed back tooffset some losses (sometimes all losses, depending on how deep). A covered call strategy involves a trader writes a call option on the stock they buy are orhave been detained. In addition to getting a premium for the sale, with a covered call, holders also get access to the benefits of owning an asset that underlies all the way up to the strike price, at which the shares will get called. This strategy consists of written call is covered by a long stock position equivalent. This gives small hedge on the stock and allow investors to earn premium income, in return while sacrificing a lot of upsides potential of stocks.

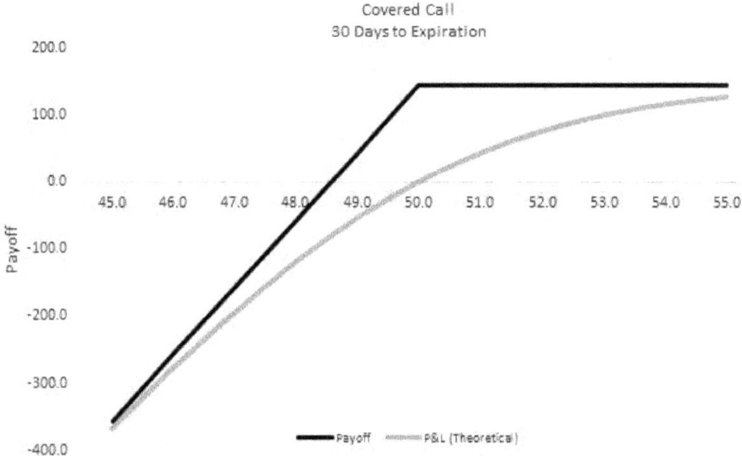

Which traders use this strategy?

The investors call is covered using this strategy and is looking for stock prices steady or increased slightly during the option term at least. This strategy is not suitable for very bearish or very bullish investors. Some investors will execute this strategy once they've seen a nice profit on the exchange. Often, they will sell out-of-the-money call, so if the stock price rises, they are willing to part with stocks and took profits. A covered call can also be used to achieve revenue above and beyond stock dividend. Interest in case it is for the option expires worthless.

Trader discusses best to call a shareholder is perfectly willing to sell the shares if the stock rises, and the call is assigned. Shareholders who would be reluctant to part with the stock, mainly mid-rally, typically not candidates for this strategy. A covered call requires close monitoring, and a readiness to take prompt action if a task that should be avoided during the sharp rally;even then, there are no guarantees.

How to effectively use this strategy to generate profits

Write (i.e. selling) call generates income in the form of premiums paid by the buyers' choice. And if the share price remained stable or increased, then the author will be able to maintain this income as profit, although profit might have been higher if there is no written summons. Because, in equilibrium gifts on a covered call position is the same as short put position, the price (or premium) must be equal to the premium of the short put or put naked.

A covered call writer can choose a

higher strike price out-of-the-money and conserve more upside potential for the stock during the strategy. It requires vigilance, quick action, and may charge extra for buying a call back, especially if such stock is rising fast.

Examples of covered call strategy

Positions covered call made by buying (or have) stock and sell call options on a stock-for-share basis. In the example, 100 shares purchased (or reserved) and one call is sold. In exchange for the premium received, which provide income in sideways markets, and limited protection in a declining market, investors are giving up potential gains above the strike price of the call. Call premium increase in market revenue neutral, but the call seller assumes the obligation to sell stock at a strike price at any time until the expiration date. In a covered call position, the effect of loss is on the downside. Stock positions have a big risk because the price could decline sharply. Let assume you decided to buy 100 shares of AC Corporation for $100 per share. You also predict that the stock price of AC Corporation will grow to $105 in the next six months.

What are the advantages and disadvantages of this strategy?

Advantages of Covered Calls

Moreover, if the underlying asset price slightly declined, premiums willbe offset portion of the losses. Selling covered call options can help offset the downside risk or add to regain the upside.

The advantage is that of all the low-risk strategy available to us, if you master the covered call writing strategy, you can get the highest returns, higher than all the low-risk strategy more. Now, another one is the amount of control you have on the outcome.

Disadvantages of Covered Call.

It is not recommended using the covered call strategy if you are expecting a large appreciation of the underlying assets because of the advantage you are locked to the strike price call option. At the same time, if the price of the underlying asset is significantly decreased, the premium from selling the call will now only cover a fraction of the losses. One disadvantage is the potential for profit when you have a covered call position is limited to the strike price.

Compared with standard stock strategy, transaction costs were approximately doubled or more than doubled since the cost of option trading generally higher than stocks. To overcome this, you need to trade with enough money per position. However, the covered call, you cannot "let your profits run" because it limits your upside. If the stock rises above the strike price, the seller does not enjoy full appreciation. Sellers profit is limited to the premiumreceived plus the difference between the share purchase price and the option strike price. Option sellers cannot sell the underlying shares without first buying back the call option. A significant decline in stock prices (greater than premiums) will have adverse effects on the entire transaction. Losses due to move downwards in the underlying stock price is limited only by the amount of the premium received.

How to effectively use the covered call strategy to generate profits

These strategies result in profit or loss is determined by the purchase price of the shares, which may occur either in the past with different prices. Assume the stock and option positions acquired simultaneously. If at the end of the position is still open, and investors want to sell shares, a strategy tolose money only if the share price has fallen more than the number of call premium. The main motive is to obtain premium income, which has the effect of increasing the overall returns on stocks and provide a measure of downside protection. The strategy of using options to generate income can beas simple as selling a covered call. If you are looking for income producing strategies using options, comparing the profile risk / reward of each strategy and choose the one fits your goals, risk tolerance, time horizon and temperament.

What is the risk/reward of this strategy?

Risk of Covered Calls

There are two risks to the covered call strategy. Real risk of losing moneyif the stock price goes below the breakeven point. The bottom line is the breakeven stock purchase price minus the option premium received, and the risk of an opportunity not to participate in a large increase in stock prices.

Covered calls are limited risk, limited-reward. Limited risk is similar to owning shares, and limited reward comes from the short call premium and transaction gains that you may have. In exchange for limiting your risk, you have a better chance of profitability than playing a simple old stock. A covered call is a strategy, and risk management options that involve holding a long position in the underlying asset (e.g., shares) and sell (write) call option on underlying asset.

Call seller must continue to stock or the underlying contract, or they will be holding a naked call, with potential loss is theoretically unlimited if the underlying security rises.

Protective Put

When a put option is used to protect another pre-existing financial position on the same asset (or bought simultaneously with the option) is called a protective put.

The objective in this case is to limit the maximum downside in thefinancial position to be hedged with the put.

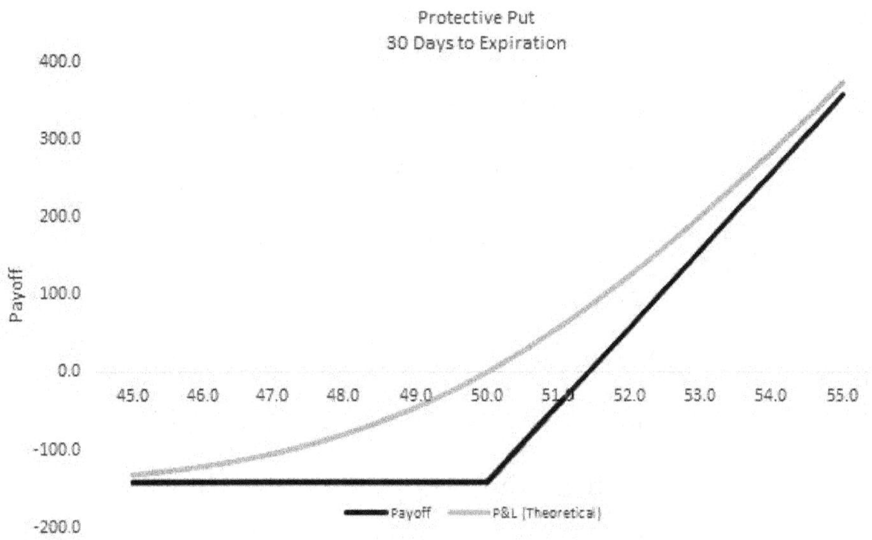

Chapter 12: Long Positionor Neutral strategy?

The beauty of market-neutral strategies like the covered call and the collar is that they are conservative by nature and yet are powerful in terms of the returns they generate. You don't need to do anything fancy beyond learning a few technical-sounding names to impress others at cocktail parties!A well-executed collar will pre-define your maximum gain and loss in advance. This way, you know exactly what will happen if the market behavesin a certain manner and can rest knowing that no matter what happens, your risk is defined fully and you need not worry about slippage or volatility.

Do note that there is the possibility of loss. The covered call does nothave this component to it, but the collar does. Hence, the collar is the first strategy we'll deal with where defining your risk per trade becomes important. While I don't like putting a number of strategies, you can conservatively expect around 10-12% per year with the collar strategy.

This might sound like it's not worth it given that a basic index fund has returned the same over the years. Well, consider that this is a market-neutral strategy, so you're insulated against up and down movements, unlike in an index fund. Second, index fund data is averaged over eighty years. Within those stretches, there have been decades where real returns have been negative.

Execution

The collar assumes that you have a bullish outlook on a stock. Ideally, you will want to hold the stock for at least a year since this will ensure you receive maximum tax benefits and avoid the short-term capital gains tax.

Therefore, a good idea with a collar is to buy LEAPS, which are options that expire a year out. This ensures that the trade will need minimum maintenance.

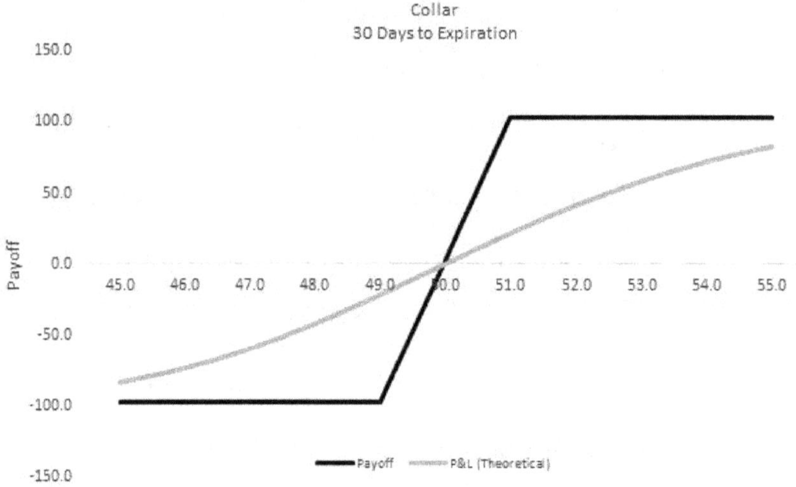

However, this is isn't really necessary as you can keep establishing the collar every month. You might be getting confused at this point so let me back up a little. The collar trade has three legs to it:

- The long stock positions
- A short out of the money call
- A long near the money put

The long stock position is established in the belief that the stock is going to go up in the long term. Your holding period could be indefinite, or for justa year, it doesn't matter. As long as you think it's going up. You could do thisfor a shorter (thirty day) period as well, but you will need to factor in the tax implications in such cases. If you're happy making a profit then frankly, taxes should not be too important to you.

Let's say you've looked at AMZN and like its prospects at $1833.51 (current market price). Sure, the market might decline a little, but you think it's going to hit $1980 eventually and you would like to profit from this movement with minimal risk. So, you first establish your long position and buy, let's say 100 shares of AMZN at current prices. Your long stock investment is $183,351.50.

Next, you want to establish the short call, which will give this trade the look of a covered call.

Once this is done, you need to establish the long put, which is close to the money. The idea is that the put covers your downside risk, much as a stop- loss order would. You think AMZN is unlikely to go below $1825 thanks to the presence of significant support and decide to buy this put.

The ask on the 1825 near month put is $49.60 or $4960 per contract. So, let's work out the math here:

Your total cost per share= long stock position- short call position + longput position= 1833.51-9.55+49.6= $1873.56 per share.

Your maximum loss per share = Long stock purchase price- long put strike price + Short call premium earned = 1833.51 - 1825 + 9.55 =

$18.06/share

Your maximum gain per share = Short call strike price - long stock purchase price - long put premium paid = 1980-1833.51-49.6 = $96.89/share

Reward to risk ratio = 5.3X

Here's where risk management comes into play. You know your maximum loss before you even enter the trade. So, all you need to do is to ensure that the maximum loss is within your designated risk per trade percentage. In this example, your trading account size will need to be large and at least $91,000, but this is because of the costly premiums on AMZN stock.

Given the risk-free nature of the collar though, you can safely increase your risk per trade to 8% or even 10%. The caveat is that your analysis of the stock needs to be correct and sound. As such, I do not recommend beginners do this. There is another option you could try.

If you choose to speculate in cheaper stocks, you can operate pretty successfully in this manner with lesser capital. Please note: I'm not including the cost of the long stock position in your trading capital since this is an investment position. If you wish to speculate for the short term, you'll need this capital as well.

So here we have a downside of the collar strategy. While it is largely risk-free, it does need a lot of money to pull off.

Leveraged Collars

In lieu of this hurdle, what you can choose to do is to deploy a leveraged collar. The costliest portion of the collar is the long stock position. If your analysis is solid, then you can easily leverage this portion of the trade and boost your return on equity. If you have access to 50% leverage, which is quite common, your return on equity effectively doubles.

This is a great choice if your technical analysis is spot on or if you've

spotted the stock headed into an extremely strong support level from which itmust bounce. Stocks which are in a large range are also excellent candidates for this strategy, and you can place the call and the put on either side of the range boundary. If none of this made sense to you.

For now, consider that choice of leverage. Of course, one of the things you must always consider is what to do if the trade doesn't work out.

Adjustment

Let's say that the stock dips and brings your put into the money. At this point, your long stock position is in a loss, your long put is in a profit, and you've already earned the premium on the short call. For better illustration, let's say the market price is now $1820, which is $5 below the strike price of our put and is $13 below the stock purchase price.

They put caps your maximum loss to $1825 or to $8 per share, so you need not worry about the stock crashing down. One thing I want to highlight here is that premiums of the call and the put will have changed. The ask on the call would have decreased by at least $5 since this represents the intrinsic value lost by the price dip.

The put would have increased by the same amount as well. So, it's price will now be at least $54.60 (49.6+5). Your choices are as follows:

1.Take the maximum loss and move on

2.Adjust the collar downwards

If you think your original analysis was wrong and that AMZN is not going to go up, then you take option number one and move on to other opportunities. However, if you're convinced that your analysis was correct and that this downward movement is a fake out, then you can choose option two.

To adjust the collar, first, you sell your put and cover (buy back) your call and the profit on this will be at least $10 per share. Next, you establish a collar at lower prices. So, you buy another put with a strike price near the money to the current, decreased market price and write a call which is either at the same profit target level or at a new, lower one.

This way, you've profited from the market's downward movement in terms of realized gains and are still in your longer-term collar trade. This is what makes options trading so powerful. If you had used a simple stop-loss order for a directional trade, your trade would have ended once the market dipped.

However, you have made an additional $10 per share profit on this trade, although the market went against you. It's safe to say that this is taking advantage of both worlds.

The only point of concern would be in terms of leverage. If you've leveraged your long stock position, then the decline in price will put pressure on your maintenance margin. This is why you need to keep your risk low orto manageable levels. The decline from $1833.50 to $1820 is only 0.07%, butthe loss on your capital (unrealized) is many multiples of that.

Therefore, if you're going to leverage your capital either have enough experience analyzing markets well enough to make educated calls on it froma technical perspective or limit your risk drastically by reducing your risk per trade to less than 1%. How low should you go? Well, as low as an amountthat doesn't keep you up at night. It takes some time to switch from thinking of losses in terms of amounts to percentages.

So take your time playing around with which level fits you best. When in doubt err on the side of caution.

Chapter 13: Beginners Common Mistakes

Trading is not an easy thing. Most of you do not know that. You just start the business with no plans, tips, and strategies. How do you even expect to survive? Entering into the options trading game with so much excitement, forgetting the crucial things you need to do will lead you nowhere. Mistakes eventually arise, and you become stranded on what to do. You will be informed of some of the mistake's traders commit and the ways you can shunfrom those mistakes.

Common Options Trading Mistakes

There are several common mistakes that traders commit while trading options. Below is a detailed list you can go through it.

Lacking a trading plan.

Most traders enter into the options trading game without a plan. You have got a high potential for loss. Failure to organize you into trading is preparing to fail. Without guidelines, you cannot make it in trading. All your goals of making money will be destroyed. When you buy or sell that option, you will be incurring a lot of losses.

Lacking an exit strategy.

When your plans fail to work out, what do you do? Do you just implement rushing decisions on your trading? An escape plan comes in handy here. Having an exit plan is very crucial in all trading. You can control your profits and losses. Most traders fail to have a detailed escape plan, which makes them fail tremendously. You lose all your money and fail in trading.

Having ignorance at the time of expiry.

Options have a date of expiration. It is an important factor when purchasing calls and buying put options. Most traders fail to recognize this factor and end up messing up the last minute. Options lose their value when you are closer to the time of expiration.

Buying options with the mentality that they are cheap.

Cheap is expensive. Cheap options have lower premiums compared to the expensive ones. You will earn little or no cash with cheap options with many losses. Options that are out of the money are not friendly at all, especially for beginners in options trading.

Selecting the wrong trade.

Working on a trade that you cannot handle can land you into big trouble. There is a high potential for bigger risks.

Work on the trade you can manage to succeed. Putting effort into complex stuff than your ability is a totalfailure. Many traders who get themselves on the wrong trade lose a lot of their money and precious time.

Depending on guesswork.

Too much guesswork in options trading is a risky game. Guesswork like the rise and fall in the stock's price is not an advisable strategy. You should take advantage of the tools of research, analysis, and education materials. Tools for analysis help in analyzing outcomes in a detailed manner as compared to guesswork. Education materials will empower your knowledge a lot in trading, and you will be aware of the basic concepts. The research tool will assist in the formulation of strategies to be used in trading. The use of guesswork will surprise you a lot with the trading failures.

Ignoring protective stop loss.

Failing to have a stop loss is a really bad idea. You can fail tremendously in trading. Most traders, who prefer to cheap options, wait to go out of the market when the option becomes fruitful, or it declines when it reaches the time of expiration.

Being over-optimistic.

Optimism is always acceptable though being over-optimistic is another bad idea. Options trading are all about performing some mathematical calculations and coming up with the right figures for your returns and losses. Putting a positive mind always is not healthy in trading since many risks are involved here. You need to be prepared for the losses that might occur and be ready enough to handle them.

Using only one strategy.

There exists some information about the many strategies you can implement in options trading. You need to go through the many strategies before deciding you will settle on which strategy. You not advised to rely on only one strategy. Having different strategies will help a lot. In case one trading strategy fails yet you are in a critical situation, you can implement another successful strategy as quickly as possible. Your trading will experience no delay. You should consider mostly the simple and crucial strategies that are needed to be implemented in all options trading. An example of the strategies is the covered call strategy.

Trading with a bigger bite.

What's all with the rush? A successful money-making procedure requires smaller and sure moves other than big and weak moves. Take your time in trading and go at the right speed. Do not be so greedy for the money that you make complex decisions ending up losing everything. Good things take time. You need to accept that fact. When you utilize much of your cash, there are higher chances of bigger losses other than just spending a little money.

Lacking persistence and consistency.

Trading is not like any other business that makes a huge amount of money just in the few days after entering the business. First and foremost, trading is tough and risky. You need to persist with all the risks and also be consistent. Most traders give up when there are occurrences of risks in trading. Keep pushing hard and of course, everything will work out fine.

Failing to accept uncertainties.

All markets have imperfections. Failure to accept the things you cannot control in options trading is a big loss. Market uncertainties will always be there, be ready to accept them and look for something else that you can control to save your time and money. Worrying a lot into something not useful is not advised in options trading.

Lacking trading goals.

"By the time the year ends, I want to have…" These are the kinds ofgoals all options traders need to have. Who out there works out for thingswith no goals? Goals are the things we wish to have or do. Failure to have clear and realistic goals in options trading is a turn off to being successful in options trading. You need to have goals that you are working for. Traderswho lack goals do not have the motivation to achieve something greater. Most of them do things for the sake of doing it. They trade at any time anduse their money recklessly. Lacking goals leads to the failure of the options trading.

How to Avoid Common Mistakes

Mistakes are always in the game. You need to find yourself some strategies and ways to survive in options trading. Mistakes are part of the learning process. You should learn from your mistakes for growth and improvement the next time you are trading.

Do not be emotional when you commit mistakes in options trading.

You will get carried away by the emotions and end up doing things of no importance. Go through your mistakes and see where you went wrong. Put much effort next time and avoid the mistakes to succeed.

Below is a detailed list of some of the ways on how to shun fromcommon mistakes in options trading

Possess an options trading plan. Test the plan after formulating it. If it works, it is well and good. Stick to it. It helps in organizing your trading patterns. You will be able to estimate your profits and losses. A trading plan makes you disciplined and responsible for trading. You will know yourmoves during your worst-case scenarios while trading options. Implement your working strategies according to the plan.

Work with a different and reasonable number of strategies. Do not rely on one strategy. It is dangerous. Arm yourself with several successful and crucial options trading strategies to be on the safer side when market imperfections decide to play along. Strategies assist you on how to do your things in trading and provide protective measures.

Take good advantage of technical tools provided to you by your broker. They enhance a quick understanding of options trading and understanding the basic concepts. They also ease the trading process since most of the trading platforms are online software.

Do not spend much money when placing trades, especially when you are a beginner. Begin from a small amount since the risks involved here are minimal. Do not utilize all your cash when you are a newbie only to end up losing everything. Take care of your money since you worked hard for it.

While trading, utilize the disposable income that can easily be refunded. Do not reach for your school fees or money for food. The risks involved in options trading are huge; it is tough to refund the money you lost. Using the money for food to placing trades will lead to starving and lack of school fees. Be wise when dealing with this trading.

You need to have realistic and achievable goals that you want to accomplish when starting off options trading. Goals are there to motivate you in trading. You will always put effort into trading to succeed what you desire.

Enter into a trade that you can manage. Many individuals will mislead you on the internet on the types of trades. Stick to your plans and select the types of trades good for you. Getting yourself into many and complex trades will stress you a lot.

There are different types of options such as binary options and many others.

You should decide on the type of option

you will settle with. Do not be the trader who deals with everything. Things will go out of control and you will lose everything. Decide on the option you more interested in and perfect that skill on the market.

Traders should be serious with the factor of time of expiration. The time of expiry is related to the value of an option. You should be alert and select options with a longer duration to expiry for your option to have a high value. You will be able to gain profits and massive returns.

Consider volatility in the market. It will save you from a lot of trouble in the market. The metric, implied volatility, can tell how volatile the market will be in the future. The metric can tell the amount of options premium you are capable of generating. You should, therefore, make use of the implied volatility in options trading.

Practice a lot in options trading. Have a routine of when to place your trades on the platforms. Study more on the best time to perform your type of trades in the options trading market. Practice will make you get used to trading with time which is a tip for successful options trading.

Have an escape plan for yourself. Do not start trading without an exit plan. This strategy saves you from losses when the market is experiencing worst-case scenarios. It guides you on the actions to implement at dark times which are better than the closure of a business.

Buying not-cheaper options are preferred to sticking to only cheaper options. Cheaper options have no progress in trading; they have lower options premiums as compared to the expensive ones. You should buy good options to earn more. Check on the quality of the options before purchasing.

Tends using protective measures in options trading. Measures such as covered call strategy assisting in protecting your trading capital and prevents you from risks in trading.

Chapter 14: Options Strategies

The next thing we need to look at is some of the different strategies you can use when you want to trade-in options. Everyone needs to enter the market with some good strategies ahead of time. This makes it easier forthem to make sure they enter the market at the right times, and that they can pick the right times to exit the market as well.

The Long Call

This is a strategy that bets the asset will rise above the strike price before the expiration date. If you look at the underlying asset and the market andyou think the price will rise before the options contract ends, then the long call is a good one to use.

If you do this call well, then the upside on this call can provide you with an infinite amount of profits until the expiration, as long as that asset sees an increase in the price. Even if you see that the stock is moving in the wrong way, it is possible to salvage at least part of the premium that you have by selling the call before it expires. The downside is a complete loss of the premium paid if the stock does not go up or if it starts to go down, but this is less risky than purchasing the stock outright.

The Long Put

The long put is going to be worth the most when you see the stock reaches $0 per share, so the maximal value will be the strike price times 100 times the number of contracts that you decide to do. You also get the benefit that if the price of the asset goes up, you can still sell the put and then save up some of the premium, as long as you still have a bit of time before your expiration. The most you can lose is all the loss of your premium based on how much you spend.

The reason that we want to use this one is that the long put is a good way to wager on the asset declining. If you are able to stomach that you may potentially lose the whole premium, you can do this one. If you do see a big decline in that asset, then you will earn more with the puts than you would byshort-selling that stock.

The Short Put

The short put is basically seen as the opposite of the long put. Theinvestor will sell their put, or they will go short. With this one, the investor is betting that the stock will stay flat, or it will continue to rise until it reaches the expiration date. Remember that with this one, the other person is betting the price will go down and you hope it doesn't. Like the long call, this short put can be a wager on a stock rising, but it has some big differences that go along with it.

While a long call will bet that there will be a big increase in the value of a stock or other asset, the short put is going to be more modest and can pay off more modestly, though it can work in some situations.

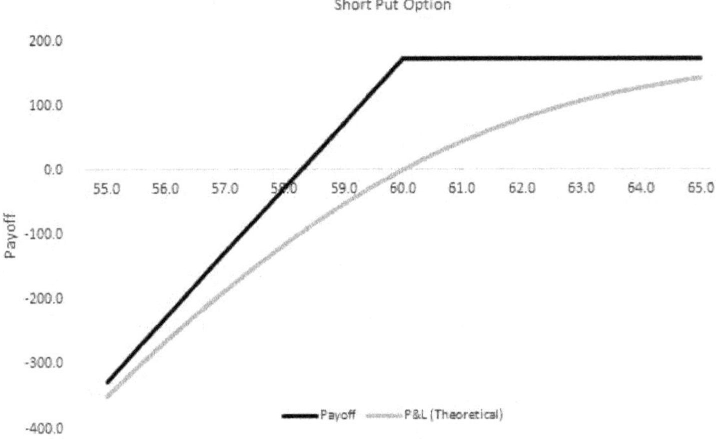

Covered Calls

The first thing that we want to look at is the covered call. This is a good strategy because it will help to reduce your risks of being all alone on a stock that is long while making sure you can get some income in the process.

The trade-off that we will get with this one is that you need to be willing to sell off the shares you have at a price that is set, which will be the short strike price. Not sticking with this will cause you to lose money in theprocess. To help you execute this one, you need to purchase the underlying stock on the options contract, just like we talked about before. Then at the same time, we need to write, or sell, one of the call options on that exactsame share.

Married Put

We can then move on to the second type of strategy that we can usewithin our options, and this one is known as the married put. In this strategy, the investor will purchase an asset, such as some shares of a chosen stock. And then, at the same time, they will purchase the put options for the same number of shares in that same stock. The holder of the put option will then have the right to sell, within the time limits of the option, to sell the stock using that strike price, no matter what the value of the stock is all about.

The reason that you, as an investor, would use this one is that it can help to protect them against any downside risk when they hold onto the stock. Then this strategy will work just like an insurance policy and will help to establish the price floor if the price of the stock decides that it wants to turn and fall quickly.

Bull Call Spread

Now we can move on to a great strategy to learn about because it works well with options and in the stock market if you decide to purchase the stocks outright. With this strategy, known as the bull call spread, the investor is going to buy calls of an asset at a specific strike price, and then at the same time they will also buy the same number of calls, but at a strike price that is higher. Both of these will come with the same asset, so don't try to do it with two different ones, and they will have the same expiration with them.

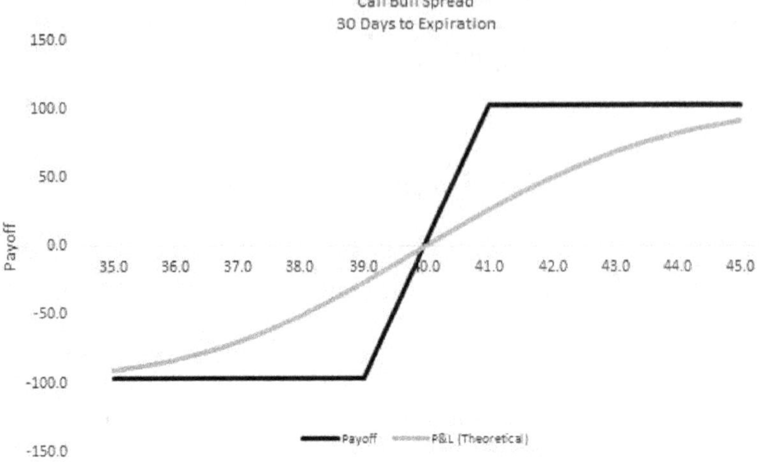

Bear Put Spread

We spent some time talking about the bull call spread and how to use it when we think the market is bullish. But there are times when the market willgo in the opposite direction, and we will end up with a bearish marketinstead. This is why working with a bear put spread could be the best option to help you out here.

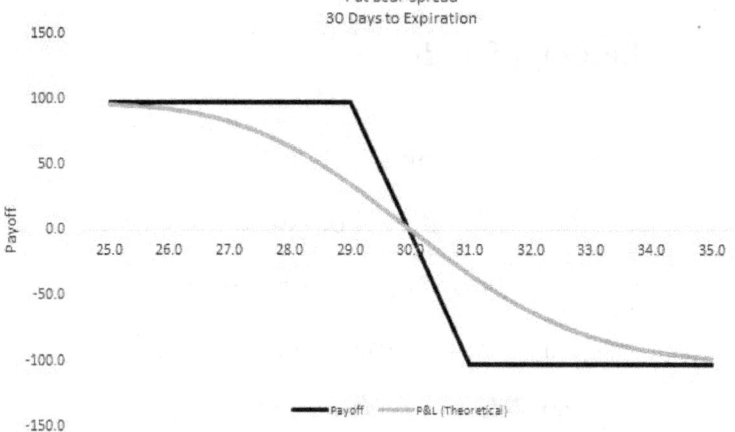

Protective Collar

Sometimes it is a good idea to find ways to protect yourself in the market.It would be nice if the stock market, or any other underlying asset that youuse with options, would follow a pattern that made sense and always stayed the same. But if that happened, then everyone would get into the market, and you would not be able to make the money that you want. The good news is the protective collar strategy will be able to help you get this done, ensuring you are protected in the market.

The Long Straddle

You can't look much at the world of investing without looking at some ofthe straddle options that are out there. This is a great strategy that you can usethat will provide you with lots of choices and can make it easier for you to stay protected and make as much money as possible. And we are going to spend some time looking at how to complete what is known as a longstraddle.

The long straddle strategy will be one where the investor is able to purchase the put and the call option at the same time. You want to do this with the same asset underneath the option, with the same strike price and the same expiration date. Everything has to be the same on this one, except that you do one put option and one call option.

The Long Strangle

In the long strangle strategy, the investor will spend their time working onan out of the money call option, while also going through and doing an out of the money put option at the same time. We need to make sure the underlying asset of both is the same and that we keep the expiration date the same as well. This can help you to protect yourself if you are not certain which direction the market will go.

Long Call Butterfly Spread

This is a fun one that allows you to stay in the market a bit longer and can make it easier for you to really see some results with what you are doing here. However, we have to make sure that we use it well and that we are getting in and out at the right parts along the way. The strategy we will talk about here is known as a long call butterfly spread.

All of the other strategies we have taken a look at so far in this guidebook were a combination of two contracts or two positions. With this one, though, we will want to use the call options. With this one, the investor will combine both the bear spread, and the bull spread strategies that were earlier in this guidebook. You would also need to make sure you work with three strike prices that are different. You will still stick with the same expiration date and the same underlying assets along the way to make this happen.

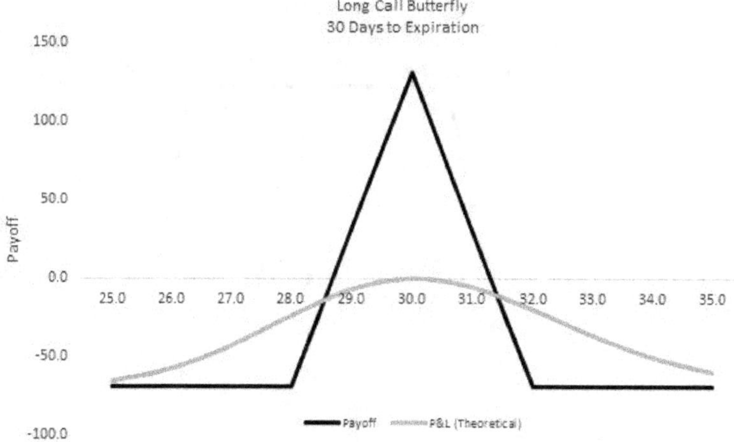

Iron Condor

The next choice that we are going to add to our list is known as the iron condor. This one is really interesting and allows us to work on a lot of different things at once to see some results.

The way to construct the iron condor is to sell one of your out of the money puts, and then we go through the process of selling one out of the money call while also buying one out of the money call, making sure we do this last one at a higher strike price.

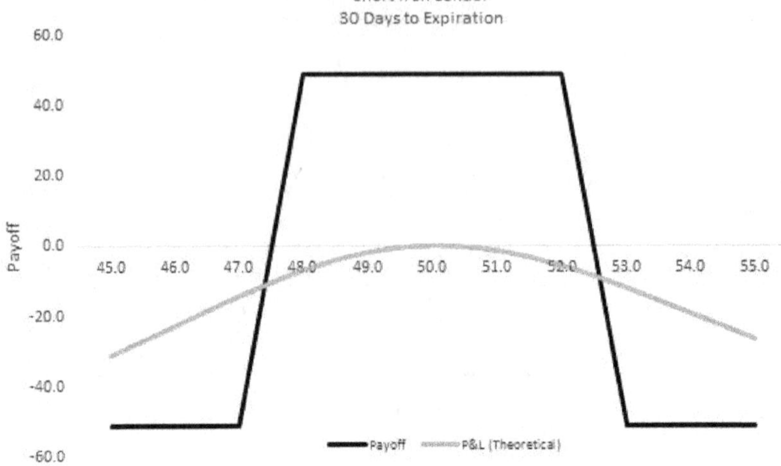

Iron Butterfly Strategy

Then it is time to move on to a strategy that is known as the iron butterfly strategy. We talked about the iron condor and the butterfly spread, so now weget to have some fun and work with the strategy of the iron butterfly. Tomake this one work, the investor will need to sell one of their at the money puts and then they can buy an out of the money put, while also taking the time to sell one of them at the money calls and purchasing an out of the money

188

call. This is a lot of steps, so make sure you really know the market and how it is supposed to work before you start.

Chapter 15: How to Start

Dozens of strike prices and expiration dates are often available for each activity, which can be a challenge for beginners. The variety of options available can sometimes make it difficult to find a suitable option for trading.**Find the right option.**

Let's say you have already identified a financial asset as stocks, commodities or ETFs that you wish to trade with options. Regardless of the selection method, there are six steps to finding the right option after identifying the underlying asset to be negotiated:

1. Formulate your investment goal.

2. Determine the payment of the risk/return.

3. Check the volatility.

4. Identify the events.

5. Develop a strategy.

6. Set the option parameters.

The six steps follow a logical thinking process that simplifies choosing a specific option for trading. Let's summarize what each of these steps entails.

1. The target of the option

The starting point for investment is your investment objective, and the trading options are no different. What goal do you want to achieve with your options trading? Is it speculative or bearish speculating on the underlying? Or should you cover the potential downside risk of a security in which you holda significant position?

Do you use trade to generate income from option premium sales? For instance, is the strategy part of a hedged call for an existing shareholder position, or do you want to hold shares? The use of income-generatingoptions is entirely different from buying speculation or hedging options.

Your first step is to develop the trading objective as the basis for the next steps.

2. Risk/Return

If you are a conservative investor or trader, you cannot find aggressive strategies like writing or purchasing a large amount of money deep (OTM) options. There is a defined risk and award profile for each optional strategy. Make sure you fully comprehend it.

3. Monitor the volatility

Implied volatility is one of the critical factors in the option price. Find out, therefore, the implicit volatility of the options. This is a crucial factor in defining the trading strategies/options, demonstrating the level of volatility indicated by the past stock volatility and the level of volatility on the broad market.

Implied volatility indicates whether other traders expect stocks to move actively or not. High implied volatility will increase premiums and make writing a more attractive option, provided that the trader does not expect volatility to expand further (which could increase the likelihood of exercising the option). Implied low volatility means cheaper option rewards, which is good for buying options when an operator expects the underlying stocks to move enough to add value to the options.

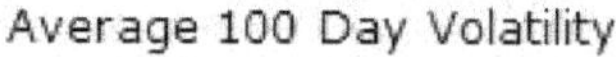
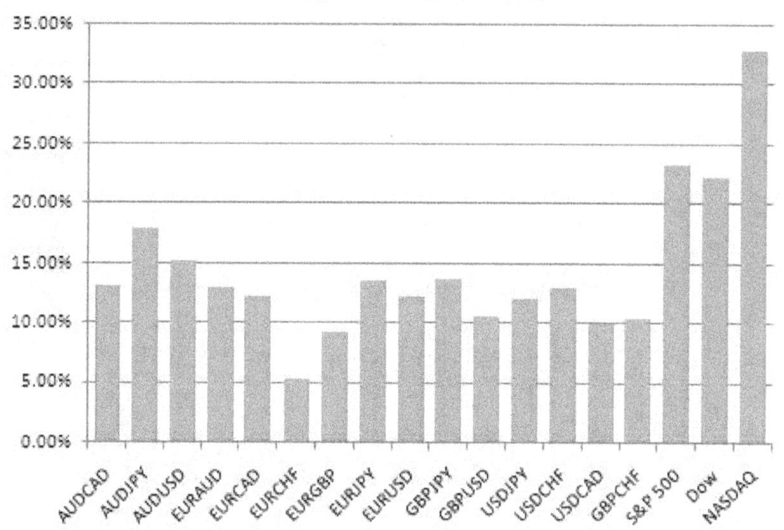

4. Identify the events

The events can be divided into two main categories: market level and market-specific. Market-level events are those that affect large markets, such as Federal Reserve Communications and Economic Data Release. Specific stock exchange events include earnings reports, product launches and spin- offs.

An event can make a significant impact on the implied volatility before it happens, and when it happens, it can have a considerable influence on the share price. Want to take advantage of the uncertainty boost before a significant incident or just wait for things to relax?

Detecting events that can affect the underlying asset can help you determine your options trading period and expiry day.

5. Develop a strategy

You now know the desired risk/return payment based on an analysis inthe previous steps, the level of implicated and historical volatility and significant events that could affect the underlying asset. It is easier to identifya specific option strategy by going through the four steps.

For example, let us say that, before companies start to report their quarterly profits, you have conservative investors who have significant stock holdings and want to receive premium income. This ensures that a covered call option that includes any or all of your portfolio securities can be opted for.

You have the choice of buying positions on the key stock indices if you are an aggressive investor who likes long waters and believes that the markets will decline sharply in six months.

6. Set the parameters

Once you have identified the specific option strategy you want to implement, set options parameters such as expiration dates, strike prices and option deltas.

Examples with these steps

Here are 2 hypothetical examples in which different types of operators are using the six steps.

Suppose a cautious investor owns 1,000 McDonald's shares and is concerned that the stock will fall by more than 5 percent in the coming months. The investor wants not to sell the share but to guard against possible declines: The investor wants:

- Objective: to cover the downside risk in the current share of McDonald's (1,000 shares); The stock (MCD) is trading at $ 161.48.

- Risk/Reward: the investor does not care about a small risk as long as it is quantifiable, but is not willing to take the unlimited risk.

- Volatility: now the share has standard trade volumes. Expectations are on increased volatility in next month.

- Events: the investor wants coverage that goes beyond McDonald's earnings report. The result comes out in just over two months, which means that the options are expected to extend by about three months.

- Strategy: Buy aims to hedge the risk of a fall in the underlyingsecurity.

- Option parameters: three-month puts with an exercise

price of $ 165are available for $ 7.15.

Because the investor wishes to cover stock over profit, he purchases $165in three months' worth. The total cost of hedging 1,000 shares of MCD is $7.150 ($7.15 x 100 shares per contract x 10). These costs exclude commissions.

If the stock remains unchanged and trades are fixed at $ 161.48 shortly before the expiration of the puts, the puts would have an intrinsic value of $3.52 ($ 165-161.48), which means that the investor will have about $ 3,520 of the amount invested in the put could be put back into position to close the position.

If the share price exceeds $ 165, the investor benefits from the increase inthe value of the 1,000 shares but loses the $ 7,150 paid for the options.

•Objective: to purchase speculative

calls from Bank of America. The stock is trading at $ 30.55.

•Risk / Reward: Investors don't mind losing their entire $ 1,000 investment, but they want to get as many options as possible to maximize their potential earnings.

•Volatility: the implied volatility for the OTM call options is 16.9% for one-month calls and 20.04% for four-month calls. Market volatility, measured by the CBOE volatility index (VIX), is 13.08%.

•Events: none, the company has just made a profit so that it will take a few months before the next profit announcement. The investor is not currently interested in earnings but expects the stock market to increase in thecoming months and believes that this stock will perform particularly well.

•Strategy: buy OTM calls to speculate on a share price

increase.

- Parameters option: four-month calls, $ 32 to BAC are available for $ 0.84 and four-month calls, $ 33, are offered for $ 0.52.

Since the investor wants to buy as many cheap calls as possible, he chooses the $ 33 four-month calls. Without commissions, 19 contracts are purchased or $ 0.52 each for a cash cost of $ 988 (19x0, 52x100 = $ 988) plus commissions.

The break-even point for trading is $ 33 + $ 0.52 or $ 33.52. IMPORTANT: if the stock expires beyond $ 33.01, it is cash, has value and is subject to automatic exercise. However, calls can be closed at any time before the deadline through a closing transaction.

Note that the strike price of $ 33 is 8% higher than the current stock price.

The investor must be confident that the price can rise by at least 8% over the next four months. If the price at maturity does not exceed the strike price of $33, the investor has lost $ 988.

While the wide range of strike prices and expiration dates can make it difficult for an inexperienced investor to get involved in a particular option, the six steps described here follow a logical thinking process that can be helpful when choosing an options trading. Define your goal, evaluate risk/return, consider volatility, consider events, plan your strategy, and define the options' parameters.

Chapter 16: Money Management

Start with a diversified basis

Leonardo Da Vinci stated in the famed Wolf of Wall Street movie: "Simplicity is the ultimate sophistication." A good portfolio excels in a good diversification strategy. A portfolio does not have to contain 30 items, but a correctly balanced mix that keeps risk and returns in balance. Or, as John Templeton said: "Diversify. In stocks and bonds, as in much else, there is safety in numbers." There is plenty of options: from gold, over ETFs, to real estate, currencies, index funds or shares. Create a clear portfolio where you,as an investor, know how to deal with the risk.

Build in a buffer for yourself

Investing is never without risk. The risk-free investment does not pay off;it only costs money. To avoid jeopardizing your healthy financial situation, put some money aside in advance. We usually assume that six months offixed costs is enough to bridge worse times. If there are indispensable opportunities in the financial markets, you can still use part of this capital to participate. Do estimate whether these opportunities are worth your buffer.

Search for the adventure and discover

If there is still some financial breathing room, you can still look for the adventure. A more aggressive investment means more risk but also a potentially greater return. Again, you can limit the risk here by diversifying. As they say about the channel: "Don't put all your eggs in one basket."

Limit losses and cash your winnings

Every investor experience it sometimes. You have a fantastic share inyour portfolio, and week after week, it performs better. And suddenly there isa turning point, you have hope for recovery, but the decline continues. Untilit gets to a phase where you get to make decisions. If you are not prepared to undergo such a rollercoaster, then be wise. Is your investment doubling? Then sell half and secure your investment. When you purchase a share, you can work with a stop-loss order. A percentage of 20 percent is common.

This means an automatic sale when the acceptable limit of loss has been exceeded. It limits your loss and allows you to reinvest with your new capitalin what will hopefully become a more successful business. A perfect strategy does not exist because you may have to grind and watch how the stock wins again after the sale. A strategy that helps to start investors to keep their night's sleep.

View the total financial picture

Making a profit on an investment is quite a pleasant feeling. But investments are not alone, not on an island, or floating in a vacuum. Investments are part of your total financial life. Many asset managers give their clients wise advice: you have to manage your accounting as a business.

That may mean that you have to monitor your debt ratio properly. For example, some investors try to counter a lesser investment with a more robust (and often riskier) investment in the hope of making up for one misconception with an absolute jackpot.

With that, they naturally run even more risk while this wasn't necessary—a sad side effect for someone who loses sight of his total accounting. Slowly trying to solve the debts of that misconception and at the same time, creating an emergency fund would certainly be a more solid approach to the problem. In this way, you create a sustainable solution, and you learn from a mistake while correcting it. It is especially important to have a sound financial basis before you venture into the stock market. Every other aspect of that personal financial accounting must be perfect.

Feel comfortable with your investment

Many people who invest and invest today grew up in a different spirit of the times. Thirty years ago, it was fashionable to get as much return as possible. Thanks to the internet, the declining pensions and changes in the banking landscape, a lot has changed over time. Modern investing and investing are mainly focused on risk and no longer on returns. Most people who invest because of a supplementary pension are focused on avoiding losses instead of making big profits. So, their hope is not to become rich or richer per se, but to have enough capital in their old age to survive.

The stock market is not a casino

Whoever plays poker knows that "all-in" already dare to pay all. You bet all your money on one game in the hope of surviving or winning the jackpot. Don't count on that opportunity when you talk about the stock market. To go all out on a single stock with all your money is never a good idea. Even the most experienced stock traders diversify their portfolio to minimize losses. In recent times, many interesting IPOs have sprung up. Although the attraction is very high among investors and investors, the lion's share among them is aware that this is not the best choice. Novice investors are often blinded by the atmosphere, the hurray mood, and the influence of others. Therefore, always realize that you do not play with money; you invest it for a specific purpose in mind.

Investing is not a hobby

Don't get us wrong: investing can be incredibly fun, but you cannot viewit as a non-binding hobby. Of course, big banks see investing as a very competitive business. That's why it's best to look at your portfolio through the eyes of a professional. It is important to understand your portfolio well, understand where your profit but also loss comes from. You must also be able to understand the companies in which you invest. Once you have completed this entire process, everything becomes so much easier. "Will this investment or investment earn me money, or will I tear it off?" An obvious question is not always asked.

Beginners often invest in stocks that seem attractive to them—a wrong motivation with often the wrong result. In the beginning, investing can sometimes have great similarities with gambling, and many starting investors want to understand how the stock market works. They soon realize the movements of large indexes, but the real work only starts when they take the investment fully seriously. Benjamin Graham said it a few decades ago: "You only do smart investment if you look at it as a business." Fund managers, analysts, traders, and other experts in financial centers take stock trading very seriously and so you better take up the challenge.

Financial resources

Before you start investing, you should better inform yourself about economic developments and prospects, the markets, and the shares that interest you. You don't have to look far: read the newspaper every day. Financial newspapers such as De Tijd, Financial Times, Wall Street Journal, can help you keep up with the most important issues. You can also consult financial websites such as Yahoo finance. Professional investors also use accounts on services such as Bloomberg and Reuters. Since everyone learns the same things at the same time, these may not be the places to make the distinction. And yet you should not try to follow in the footsteps of the experts too much. Some of the best-known investors, such as Peter Lynch, suggested that hints from daily life could provide more inspiration.

Form a Strategic Daily spending patterns

For example, Lynch "used" his wife's shopping habits to analyze which brands gained popularity. According to Lynch, traders and stock traders spent too much time in an artificial bubble. Peter Lynch's views are not old-fashioned. In 2012, a financial nitwit put the test to the test and succeeded in suddenly making 2 million dollars during a difficult stock market period of $ 20,000. Everything but a cold trick.

According to the amateur investor, there were clear trends in the spending patterns of women, young people, and low incomes. The man invested in shares that everyone could own and noticed trends before bankers saw them and made substantial gains.

How can you monitor your stock portfolio?

If you decide to invest in shares, drawing up an investment plan is the first step. However, once you have compiled your equity portfolio, you are not yet ready. Monitoring your equity portfolio to monitor whether it still meets your original objectives is just as important. Some investors like to check the status of their investments every day. But for many investors, thisis not desirable or necessary. In other words, monitoring your equity portfolio depends on both the type of investments in your portfolio and the type of investor that you are.

Monitor shares

The moment you have invested not in funds, but self-selected individual shares, it is interesting to monitor these continuously. The most important goal here is to check if a share still meets your initial criteria. In almost all cases, this will depend strongly on your estimate of the future expectation for the underlying company or the estimate of the stock market. Many of these estimates are based on company income. You have to monitor the changes that affect income.

Newspapers, press releases, and reports

Check the financial news and announcements about your shares daily, weekly, or monthly. This includes new products, changes in management, or news about competitors. If analysts report on your share, it is wise always to read it immediately. Since these can be of great importance for market sentiment.

Online sources of news

Many brokers allow you to monitor your stock portfolio online. In some cases, there is even a direct link to news and analysis of the relevant share. This way, you not only see at a glance how your portfolio is doing, but you also have an overview of relevant news sources that can influence the price. Many brokers offer the option to receive alerts by e-mail or text messagewhen certain developments occur on the market. Does your broker not have such an option? Then online portals like finance. yahoos allow you to enter your portfolio. After which they will provide you with a large number of relevant news sources. Both through your broker and financial websites such as Yahoo Finance, Morningstar, and Bloomberg, you will be provided with information in real-time. Since the stock market also responds to developments in real-time, this information can enable you to react promptly to developments to maximize your returns.

Chapter 17: Options Trading Psychology

Options trading is most suitable for a certain personality type and mindset. But if you are intrigued by the concept of options, but you simply have not had a chance to develop the correct mindset before, there are a few tips that we can rely on to get in the right frame of mind.

You can weather the storm

Options prices can move a lot throughout short periods. So, someone wholikes to see their money protected and not losing any is not going to be suitable for options trading. Now, we all want to come out ahead, so I am not saying that you have to be happy about losing money to be an options trader. What you have to be willing to do is calmly observe your options losing money, and then be ready to stick it out to see gains return in the future. This is akin to riding a real roller coaster, but it is a financial roller coaster.Options do not slowly appreciate the way a Warren Buffett investor would hope to see. Options move big on a percentage basis, and they move fast. If you are trading multiple contracts at once, you might see yourself losing $500and then earning $500 over a matter of a few hours. In this sense, although most options traders are not "day traders" technically speaking, you will be better off if you have a little bit of a day trading mindset.

You don't make emotional decisions

Since options are, by their nature, volatile, and very volatile for many stocks, coming to options trading and being emotional about it is not a good way to approach your trading. If you are emotional, you are going to exit your trades at the wrong time in 75% of cases. You don't want to make any sudden moves when it comes to trading options. As we have said, you should have a trading plan with rules on exiting your positions, stick to those rules and you should be fine.

Be a little bit math-oriented

To understand options trading and be successful, you cannot be shy about numbers. Options trading is a numbers game. That doesn't mean you have to drive over to the nearest university and get a statistics degree. But if you do understand probability and statistics, you are going to be a better options trader. Frankly, it's hard to see how you can be a good options trader without having a mind for numbers. Some math is at the core of options trading and you cannot get around it.

You are market-focused

You don't have to set up a day trading office with ten computer screensso you can be tracking everything by the moment, but if you are hoping to setup a trade and lazily come back to check it three days earlier, that isn't going to work with options trading. You do need to be checking your trades a few times a day. You also need to be keeping up with the latest financial and economic news, and you need to keep up with any news directly related to the companies you invest in or any news that could impact those companies. If the news does come out, you are going to need to make decisions if it's news that isn't going to be favorable to your positions. Also, you need to be checking the charts periodically so you have an idea of where things are heading for now.

Focus on a trading style

As you can see, there are many different ways that you can trade options. In my opinion, sticking to one or two strategies is the best way to approach options trading. I started off buying call options, but now, I focus on selling put credit spreads and iron condors. You should pick what you like best and also something that aligns with your goals. I moved into selling put credit spreads and iron condors because I became interested in the idea of making a living from options trading with regular income payments, rather than continuing to buy calls and hope that the share price would go up. There is noright or wrong answer, pick the trading style that is best suited to your style and needs.

Keep detailed trading journals

It's easy to fool yourself when trading options, especially if you are a beginner. I hate to make the analogy, but this is kind of like going to the casino. If you have friends that gamble at casinos, then you are going tonotice that they tend to remember the wins, and they will forget all the times that they gambled and lost. I had a cousin that won a boat, and she wasalways bragging about how she won a boat at the casino. I remember telling her that yes, she won a boat, but she paid $65,000 more than the boat was worth to the casino over the years. You don't want to get in the same situation with your options trading. It can be an emotional experience because trading options are active and fast-paced. When you have a profitabletrade, it will be exciting. But you need to keep a journal to record all of your trades, to know exactly what the real situation is. That doesn't mean you quit if you look at your journal and find out you have a losing record, what you dois figure out why your trades aren't profitable and then make adjustments.

Options traders are flexible

I have said this before, but one thing you need to remember about options trading is you can make money no matter what happens to the stock. So, you need to avoid falling into the trap of only trading options to make money one way. Most frequently, people do what they have been brainwashed to do and they will trade call options hoping to profit from rising share prices. If you are in that mindset now, you need to challenge yourself and begin trading in different ways so that you can experience making money from decliningstock prices, or in the case of iron condors, stock prices that don't even change at all. You need to be able to adapt to changing market conditions to profit as an options trader. So, don't entrap yourself by only using one method. Earlier, I said to use one or two styles, but you should be ready to branch out when market conditions change. Remember this – market conditions always change eventually. As I am writing, we are in the midst ofa long-term bull market, but it won't last forever.

Take a disciplined approach

Don't just buy options for a certain stock because it feels good. You need to research your stocks. That will include doing fundamental analysis. This isgoing to mean paying attention to the history of a stock, knowing what the typical ranges are for, stock in recent history is, and also reading through the company's financial statements and prospectus. Remember, I suggest picking three companies to trade options on for a year and also two index funds. The index funds require less research, but for the three companies that you pick, you should get to know those companies inside and out. Stick with them for ayear, at the end of each year, evaluate each company. Then decide if youwant to keep them and bring them forward into the following year's trades. If one company is not working out for you, then move on and try a different company.

Trading with LEAPS

Leaps are interesting options. They expire a year or more into the future. This is different than the short-term options that most people are trading.

LEAPS are more expensive, but they can also represent money-making opportunities. LEAPS also give you an indirect way to control stock.

Profiting from LEAPS

LEAPS have high prices because they have a lot of extrinsic value. Looking at June 18, 2021, Facebook call options, the $195 call is priced at $42.13 a share. So that represents a $4,213 options contract. According to thechart, it made 3.4% today, which isn't a huge amount, but I challenge you to find a bank or mutual fund that has a return of 3.4% per day. The open interest is 133. This meets our minimum criteria for getting involved in a trade. It's quite small compared to Facebook options that expire in the following month, but it's enough open interest that it's going to be possible toget in and out of a trade in a reasonable amount of time. The implied volatility is a solid 33%. For comparison, the $195 call that expires in three weeks is priced at $12.48.

Although LEAPS are expensive, they have a lot of potential for profits. You can get into a LEAP and if the stock makes a solid move, you can close your position and make large amounts of money. For that $195 call that expires in June 2021, the delta is 0.64. That means that even though theoption has a lot of extrinsic value since it expires a long way into the future, it's pretty sensitive to price changes in the stock that is with the option. If the share price goes up to $1, the option price will go up by $64. LEAPS don't suffer much from time decay. Theta for this option is only 0.03. If the share price goes up to $20 after an earnings call, the option is going to go up by $1,280. So you can make pretty good profits. The barrier to entry is the high price to buy one.

Poor Mans Covered Call

One of the interesting things that you can do with a LEAP is you can use it to sell covered calls. That sounds crazy, but it works. You can use the LEAP to cover call options that you sell to open. So, you can invest in LEAPS at a fraction of what it costs to invest in the stock, and then start selling calls against the options to generate income. Although it might cost $4,600 to buy a Facebook LEAP, it would cost nearly $20,000 to buy 100 shares of stock. Buying a LEAP gives you de facto control over a hundred shares of stock at a much smaller price than the investment cost.

For the price of 100 shares of Facebook, you could invest in 4-5 LEAPS, and have a lot more room to

work with as far as selling call options.
So, you could end up having a higher
income.

Chapter 18: How does Swing Trading work?

Swing trading uses technical analysis to determine whether or not particular stocks might go up or down in the very near term. Swing traders are not concerned with the long-term value of a given stock.

After Hours Trading

The equities markets in the United States usually close down at 4.00 pm eastern time. Even then, traders continue to have access to the markets until 8.00 pm in the night. Access is enabled via platforms such as ECN and exchanges such as the NYSE. Therefore, trading the markets any time after 4.00 pm till 8.00 pm in the night is referred to as after-hours trading, post market trading, or extended hours trading. The problem with this trading period is that it is very illiquid as most trading specialists and market makers avoid trading at these times.

The most outstanding feature of after-hours trading is the lack of liquidity in the market. A lot of experts consider this to be risky or even dangerous territory because there is often very little activity. Spreads are often very wide as most of the other traders, especially market makers, have left for the day. Therefore, the securities' activity is often very low. However, day traders know how to benefit from such situations. For instance, if breaking news is announced during this period, then related stocks could have significant action that can be traded.

Trading after hours is tricky due to the illiquid nature of most securities as well as the large spreads. The best time to trade after hours is only when there is a significant news item that affects a particular company or an industry. Such news is best if received during the earnings periods, which occur mostly during quarterly earnings reporting times. This kind of trading should, therefore, be left to seasoned traders only.

High-Frequency Trading

High-frequency trading, also referred to as HFT, are essentially programs that execute complex algorithms that can generate superfast trades across different markets. The purpose of these rapid trades includes arbitrage and market making. The outstanding feature here is the thin profits that accrue from the large volumes of trades initiated. Trades initiated can number intheir millions on any given day. It is said that about 50% or half of the volume trades initiated in US stock markets are HFT.

These trades rarely hold a position for long. One of the most useful ingredients in any HFT operation is low latency in order to keep the speed advantage over other traders such as retail traders. It is a modern computer algorithm that power HFTs. If well executed, such programs can generate modest to average profits for a long period of time without incurring any significant losses. There are reports of HFT firms of running for 1000 profitable days without any losses. When everything works as required, then HFT offers a great opportunity to earn plenty of money with very little risk over a long period of time.

Latency: This term actually refers to the time taken for data transmitted between two points to get to its destination. Basically, low latency refers to high speeds, while high latency means low speeds. Most investment companies invest a lot of resources in acquiring the latest, cutting-edge infrastructure and hardware necessary for processing trades at high speeds.

Algorithms: These are basically instructions set out which are to be executed once certain conditions are met. A sophisticated algorithm such as the HFC algorithm used in trade has millions of lines of code. In recent years, algorithms have become commonplace, and most traders make use of one type or another to execute their trades.

Momentum Trading

Day traders choose momentum trading simply because all the action is on the stock market momentum. This type of day trading aims at profiting from stocks that experience a price gain, especially with huge trade volumes. In momentum trading, stocks and securities are affected by factors such as margin calls, short squeezes, and stop losses, so they move in an excessive and extreme manner. The typical approach by day traders on momentum trading is to scalp profits as quickly as possible and with as much leverage as possible.

Day traders who prefer momentum trading usually trade any security that has large volatility and significant volume. These include securities that have sustained a significant rise in price and are known as high-flyers or momentum stocks. Most of the stocks suitable for this kind of trade strategy are more volatile than those of major blue-chip companies. It is this volatility that attracts momentum traders to these trades. Volatility provides a great option to capitalize and benefit from price movements and volume. Securitieswith large volumes and high volatility that feature in the news are usually the best suited to momentum trading.

Price movement: This is the hallmark of momentum day trading. Traders often make use of shorter time frame charts like the 15-minute, 5-minute, andeven the 1-minute charts. In order to manage risk, the focus should be on the immediate action with large share volumes. It is important for momentumday traders to have precision when entering and leaving the market.

Executions and charts will, in this case, carry significantly more weight compared to the fundamentals of the underlying company. Also, stories in the news carry more weight as news is often the main driver of momentum. Also, chart patterns and essential signals will help determine the best times to initiate trades.

Chapter 19: Swing OptionsTrading Strategies

The swing trading techniques are pretty simple to grasp, and this form of trading does not demand the same urgency as well as split-second decision making needed with day trading.

For many individuals, swing trading will be the best method to ease into trading, and also could help develop good habits that will serve you no matter what additional directions the future investing of yours takes you.

Swing trading is a technique of trading where you simply hold the stocks for a quick time.

Nevertheless, unlike morning trading, swing trading positions can endure between 2 days to two weeks.

The thought is that you are holding onto the stock to make money from cost changes or maybe swings. These swings in the cost change are wherethis particular style of trading gets the name of its.

What is amazing about swing trading? Effectively, different things.

For starters, swing trading is an accessible means for actually fresh traders. Even though the pace is quick, it is not up to day trading. What this means is it enables a bit more time to believe the process of yours and make educated decisions with your trades.

For many people, the fast speed of morning trading can prove somewhat overwhelming in the beginning. Swing Trading is usually an excellent entryto morning trading, along with a solid trading train on the whole.

This does not mean it is totally relaxed. Though you are just holding onto the inventory for a couple of weeks or days, therefore it provides capability income, which exceeds capturing much longer positions on trade.

Plus, because you are just holding onto the inventory for a quick period, you can utilize the market volatility and possibly get assertive income from trades in a somewhat brief window.

Usually, whenever you consider long positions, you can overlook the stock, or maybe it may be very easy to quit being persistent. Therefore, it is not hard to lose track of what is happening in the marketplace and miss your opportune moment to exit the trade. Put more bluntly; it is not hard to get sluggish with long positions.
The very short period needed in swing trading helps ensure that you
will remain on the ball about issues.
Certainly, the main goal is earning profits.
But how's that accomplished?

The aim is perfect for you to meet stocks that are poised to create a movement throughout numerous days, months, or weeks—not only hours or minutes—then record these gains by trading in the pattern.

To locate these stocks, it is your responsibility to use complex research and analysis to ensure you can find trends as well as catalysts that'll preferably improve the chances of yours of making lucrative trades.

To profit with swing trading, you have to pick stocks with movement, which will acquire your earnings while they fluctuate or maybe swing in value.

The standard design of investing is to buy low, sell high'. Simple as that's,it is probably the most conventional way to profit.

You start by identifying a stock that is gaining. You then get truly obsessed about it. You investigate the inventory, pore over its chart, survey the history, then research possible catalysts that may be impacting the stock 'smovement.

In case, throughout your research, you have noticed a stock which alsohas space to keep gaining, you can invest and hold onto the inventory for a quick time, and also figure out when you should promote therefore you can profit.

To accomplish this, you should be disciplined and consider your exit and entry before you will trade. You have got to strive for the perfect Goldilocks zone—in which you do not hold on very long, although not too light a period also.

Indeed, it is easier said than done, especially when the emotions of yours enter the manner.

You can additionally profit by pairing brief selling with swing trading. In this particular situation, you are essentially choosing the contrary trend of the buy low, sell high' solution. You are searching for stocks you can attempt to foresee dropping huge; therefore, you can profit while they go down. (To know more about small selling, check out this post.)

Whether you are seeking losers or gainers, the most crucial aspect of profiting from this is choosing the proper stocks.

Many of the greatest businesses for swing trading are all those with good industry volume. By volume, which suggests the number of stocks that are getting bought or even sold every day. For swing traders, these continual priced changes, even if by tiny quantities— could be helpful.

The marketplace likewise matters. If the industry is running in an extreme, whether it is bearish or bullish, it can prove tough. During extraordinary times, stocks are not as simple to track; the balance is not there to enable you to plot out an obvious course of action.

In a serious sector, momentum can make stocks do things that are out of the typical. It is then difficult to figure out patterns. Because I am everything about patterns, I do not believe those are ideal conditions.

Times of market balance is the very best times for profiting from this particular method. It is when you can do sound research and find out a stock's potential future and history. This lets you capture short-term motions with much more of a feeling of security.

Determining the market sentiment can prove difficult, especially to brand new traders. Nevertheless, train a lot and do more learning and experience a lot. With time it is going to become much easier.

Still unclear on the big difference between swing trading as well as day trading? Let us tackle it today since swing trading bears some similarities to morning trading; you will find numerous essential differences.

One of the leading differences is timing

In morning trading, you keep an inventory for an extremely brief period; it may be hours or minutes, but will not be greater than one day.

With swing trading, you may hold an inventory for a couple of days to a couple of weeks, or perhaps several months.

Yet another significant difference is trend recognition. This way, swing trading is even more like pattern trading, wherever you are taking a long, close look in the basic principles which fashion play into the importance of a stock, and also according to that information, keep the inventory.

With swing trading, you look at some trends playing into the stock 's worth, as well as swap, based on a mix of essential investigation and checking out the stock's action as well as chart patterns.

Swing Trading Strategies

While generally, there are endless variants of swing trading methods, many tried-and-true setups are believed to be conventional swing trading methods.

Allow me to share several of the key ones you must know.

1.) Breakouts

The 1st of the three swing trading techniques is the breakout. A breakout tactic is an approach in which you have a placement on the first aspect of the uptrend.

Below, you monitor stock, and once it's a preferred degree of volatility and movement and breaks a vital point of resistance or support (i.e., it falls injust a defined price range), you have the industry.

Assistance, opposition, and volume are crucial. Naturally, you will additionally monitor catalysts along with other factors that might influence the cost of a stock—those are crucial strategy facets.

The setup is a vital starting place to get into a trade as well as benefit from future spikes in volatility and cost swings.

2.) Breakdowns

The 2nd of the recommended swing strategies of mine is widely knownas a breakdown. A breakdown will be the complete opposite of a breakout,the place that the stock price moves under a defined support amount. With a description, the chart points for lower costs, plus you monitoring the same fundamentals.

3.) Options

Coming in 3rd, however, not least? Swing trading with options could be a very good strategy, especially if you are looking for leverage on the investment of yours.

By training trading with choices, you are getting the option' to purchase or even sell later in case some specific criteria are met in just a definedperiod. You set up a call feature or maybe a put option based on whether you are purchasing or selling.

Only dedicate yourself to the trade, in case your ideal amounts are met. Because of this peace of mind, you have to shell out down payment or an advance of sorts. In case you do not work out the option of yours inside the time window specified, you will shed this original transaction. Nevertheless,it is much less of a loss than in case you made the total investment.

Assembly of a lucrative Chart; What must you search for in a profitable chart? Let us break it down.

Shifting Averages

Moving averages are a crucial element in determining resistance and support levels. They can also enable you to figure out the present climate of the marketplace. You will find two important kinds of moving averages.

Simple moving average (SMA)

The SMA can allow you to figure out the present weather of the marketplace. Can it be bearish or bullish? You can likewise learn resistance and support levels in addition to price points, which will help you choose when and where to enter as well as exit a trade.

Exponential moving averages (EMA): This perturbation appears for direction signals. It can enable you to figure out your exit and entry points based on fashion, which will help further perfect your entry and exit points aswell as plot a clear cut trading program.

Brief Interest

Short interest can help expand the knowledge of yours before making a swing trade. It is a ratio that compares the number of floating shares on the number of shares brief.

Usually, brief interest is estimated every month, but there is simply no completely correct tool of information for this, so it is much more of a wondering game. It provides all shares that were sold brief.

And so why does that matter? Since an impressive brief interest might be a sign that the industry is trending for bearish with this particular inventory. Nevertheless, in case the stock has a low cost and an impressive smallinterest, this may be a warning sign that a quick squeeze is occurring.

In case a stock has essentially high brief interest, which may be cross-referenced with a good catalyst, this may provide you with an indication that brief sellers want to conceal themselves in this particular circumstance. This may influence the stock price.

Volatility

Searching for volatility is essential in deciding a swing trade setup. Volatility will be the responsibility to change unpredictably and rapidly,particularly for the worse.

In the stock market, volatility typically means an increased threat, meaning greater odds of a loss.

Nevertheless, danger could additionally lead rewarding; therefore, it is essential to check out a stock 's volatility along with some other factors like catalysts along with other basic information.

Chapter 20: Mindset for Swing Traders

All of us have certain limiting beliefs we employ to restrict ourselves. The crazy thing is that we have no idea what these beliefs are for the most part. This is because they lie beneath our conscious mind, in oursubconscious. These beliefs are formed primarily thanks to our childhood experiences and the environment we grew up in.

Trading is an intense activity that deals with money. In fact, the only way to determine the success or failure of your trading business is to look at how much money you've made over time. Money happens to be a very emotional topic and people have all kinds of ideas about it. Certain things you might have heard while growing up will influence how you feel and think about your results.

The fact is that all the things you've

heard and learned about money when you were a kid will cause you to make decisions which could be detrimental to your trading success. For example, if you believe money is scarce, you'll end up creating situations that confirm this belief in your life. You may find that you have trouble keeping the money you make in trading intact and that your account's equity balance fluctuates massively.

Take some time to explore what your beliefs about money and success are. The easiest way of doing this is to ask yourself what your parents toldyou about money. Did you hear statements such as 'money needs to be saved and not spent' or 'money doesn't grow on trees?' These are pretty common things one hears.

How good were your parents with money? Was it always a struggle to make ends meet? Or were they profligate with it? Almost everyone has issues with money that causes them to sabotage themselves. The key is to recognize these troublesome beliefs and then take action to rectify them. Beliefs are justthought patterns you have learned over time.

If you learned one thing you can just as easily learn another. The way to change habits is to become aware of the existence of the troublesome belief and as it rears its head, practice the action that counteracts it. Let's look at an example of how this works.

A lot of traders beat themselves up a lot over their results. They take a look at their trades and realize that there were opportunities they missed in the moment due to being too nervous and due to an inability to pull the trigger. In order to counteract this, they go to the other extreme and begin taking trades that are less than perfect, as per their system. This of course leads to even more poor results and a vicious circle is formed.

The thing to do is to understand that poor trading results over time (at least 100 trades) is a symptom and not the disease itself. If the major cause of poor results was missing out on trades due to fear of pulling the trigger, let's examine why could this be so? Is it because the trader is extremely nervous about the result of that trade? Why would they be nervous? Could it be because they believe that this result is all important and that it's a referendumof how successful they are in life?

It seems a stretch to connect the result of a single trade to this point but remember that money is at the bottom of the issue here. An inability to make money is something that will cause most people, especially men, to feel inadequate and like a failure. If you feel as if you're a failure, you're likely toavoid situations that might paint you as one or create situations that confirm this feeling. Avoiding a trade and then beating yourself up over an inability to get good results does both.

This is why trading is such a slog for so many people. They're constantly fighting the ups and downs of their emotions and think that finding a better system is the answer. The fact is that their problems have nothing to do with the trading system and everything to do with their mindset.

Write down your beliefs about money and success. What does success look like to you? Are your expectations of trading realistic? If you're expecting swing trading to be able to give you enough money to buy a Porsche within a year, it's safe to say your head is up in the clouds a bit. Trading can make you millions when done well. It's just that the way you think it will make you millions is not how it happens.

How much of a return on your money are you expecting? Before you answer, consider that the greatest stock market investor of all time, Warren Buffett, averages a 20% return over his lifetime. And he's considered to be pretty far ahead of his peers. The fact is that most institutions such as hedge funds and private equity firms will be very happy with a trader who earn anywhere from a 10-17% return on their money.

Yet, one often sees retail traders dream of turning $1,000 into a million within a year. If a professional trader could realistically achieve that sort of return, we'd have many more billionaires on this planet! What's more, every single wealthy person would liquidate the rest of their assets and invest itentirely into a trading venture. Such numbers are ludicrous.

Keep your expectations in check and don't dream of earning outsize returns with your trading capital.

Chapter 21: Conclusion

By now, you must have figured out how easy options trading is. With the information covered here plus your desire to make it in options trading, you have no option but to excel in the business. You are now better prepared to trade options using technical analysis, fundamental analysis, and other procedures. You are also ready to take opportunities as they come and have a sense of what each trade entails, from a technical view.

- An option refers to a contract that gives a buyer the authority to buy or sell an asset at a certain price within a certain period.

- Options do not represent the real value of an asset or underlyingsecurity. An option in itself is a derivative of an asset or security

- Calls give you the right to purchase an asset while puts allow you tosell an asset.

- The options market has four participants. These are the buyer of acall, the buyer of a put, the seller of a call and the seller of a put.

- The cost of an option is referred to as the premium.

- Long-term options are also known as leaps

By now, you understand that there are a good number of tools and platforms that you can use to trade options. Since the cost of options keeps fluctuating from the start date to the maturity date, you need a platform that best suits your trading and training needs. Bear in mind that each platform has its strengths and weaknesses;

therefore, you may not find one that is 100 percent effective. A good platform is one that gives you the ability to tailor your experience. Such a platform can accommodate both novice and experienced traders. A sophisticated platform can negatively impact your proficiency since you will spend a considerable amount of time trying to understand the advanced tools and features on the platform. Having the right instrument will ensure that you trade with confidence.

Of course, we could not end the discussion without mentioning financial leverage as a benefit of trading options. The leverage comes about when you are able to translate your little capital into huge gains. It arises from the fact that a percentage increase in the price of an option is relatively higher than the increase in the underlying asset. This means that the more you invest, the higher the financial leverage. With a good trading plan, you can use this concept to minimize trading risks and maximize your returns. A great advantage in options trading is that the options contract itself is already a leverage opportunity. It allows you to grow your starting capital easily. By now, you should be able to calculate the leverage of any given position using the delta value.

When it comes to options trading, patience and commitment are key. You must be able to control your emotions. Emotional trading is a risky affair. Treating options like any other business can help manage losses with ease. Making trades just because they seem good can lead you into trouble. Actually, the difference between good traders and average ones is that a goodtrader does not allow emotions to control him. When he loses, he understandsthat it is because he made a wrong move or choice and that it is not thesystem that is working against him. Good traders do not dive into unnecessary opportunities just because of feelings; they weight the options and make decisions based on what is in the trade for them. They also understand when to quit from trade even if some losses are incurred.

We also looked at some of the tips you need to employ to ensure that you succeed in most of your trades if not all. These are simple things such as collecting enough capital before you start trading, identifying a suitable trading style, and having a risk management plan. You also have known some of the mistakes most traders make when trading options and how you can avoid them.

With all this insight into the options market, you should be able to carry out a trade from start to finish, successfully. You must, however, note that the options business is not for every investor. It can get sophisticated and dangerous if you do not put the information outlined in here into practice.

By now, it is clear to you whether this is an investment you want to tryout or not. If you are into it, then you must decide the kind of trader you would want to be. You can either be a day trader, long term trader, or a short-term trader. As a day trader, you will have the advantage of making several trades that close quickly. This option is good for you if you are interested in making small profits. Otherwise, consider long-term trading that can span a period of over 30 days but with incredible profits.

Trading on options also involves choosing the underlying security that you would wish to connect your options to. This may be in the form of commodities, stock, or foreign currency. Each currency has its own characteristics, and the liquidity status also matters. Commodities are good but very volatile, currencies trade most of the time, but the prices are easily influenced by economic news items. Stocks experience a rapid change in prices overnight.

To many people, options are a complicated instrument to trade in. However, the more you learn about them, the simpler they become. With some experience, you realize that the instrument is one of the most flexible to trade in. Nonetheless, for options trading to go well, you also need to understand the basics of picking a stock, assessing market cycles and formulating investment strategies.

Since options are highly volatile, if you do not exercise caution, you may lose all your investment at one go. That is why you need specialized training such as this one before venturing into it. A good number of people that have succeeded in options trading began as stock traders. If you are already into stock trading, you will have easy time trading options due to the many similarities that exist between the two.

Lastly, it is important to note that the shorter the trading period, the higher the stress and risks involved. If you keep holding your trades through the night, you stand a high risk of losing all your capital and destroying your account. Other than this, we are glad that you have learned a new way of earning money from the financial market and understood all the traits and skills you need to make it in binary options trading. Note that theory is never effective without practice. So, in case you need to get started, it is best to identify a trading platform and put what you have learned into practice. Remember, the more you practice, the more confident you become.

www.ingramcontent.com/pod-product-compliance
Lightning Source LLC
LaVergne TN
LVHW010502200726
843506LV00013B/2498